SKITS THAT WIN

SKITS THAT WIN

BY RUTH VAUGHN

ZONDERVAN
PUBLISHING HOUSE
OF THE ZONDERVAN CORPORATION | GRAND RAPIDS, MICHIGAN 49506

SKITS THAT WIN
Copyright © 1968 by Zondervan Publishing House
Grand Rapids, Michigan

Tenth printing   1976

.

Printed in the United States of America

FOR BILLY
The little brown-eyed boy
Who holds my heart firmly
in his hand
And for whom my greatest prayer is
That he will find and follow God's Plan.

INTRODUCTION

These skits have been created with one goal in mind: to evangelize! Their purpose is not to be produced for fun, stunts or entertainment. Their goal is to lead youth to Christ!

Evangelistic skits frequently are the most effective sermons available. However, they are not designed to be the entire program. They are, instead, the beginning feature — the mood setter — the interest catcher. At the conclusion of a skit, your minister or youth leader will take charge of closing remarks and the extending of an invitation.

These skits are new! They are novel! They are absorbing! They present the challenge of salvation! They will help to evangelize your teens!

My prayer is that these skits will be as great a blessing to the youth with whom you work — as they have been to mine!

RUTH VAUGHN

CONTENTS

NO GREATER LOVE

Characters

Barabbas: a big surly man with a special gentleness for Deborah
Martha: wife of Barabbas
Deborah: blind daughter of Barabbas (age: eight to twelve years)
Judith: sister of Martha
Hidden Voice

Setting

The setting for both scenes of this skit is in the sitting room of the home of Barabbas and Martha. The setting should be as lavish as possible to indicate Barabbas' success in his ruthless trade of thievery and robbery.

Costuming

All the characters of this skit should be in Biblical dress. Judith should be dressed plainly and simply, whereas the other characters should be elaborately dressed. Deborah should indicate her blindness in the first scene with a blank stare.

Properties

In the first scene, a hair brush and a large number of gold looking coins will be needed. The second scene will require a bouquet of flowers (artificial will be fine) and a vase.

Skit

Scene I

(The scene opens with Martha dusting about the room. A knock is heard on the door. Martha goes to left exit.)

Martha: Oh, Judith! Do come in!

Judith (enters): How are you, Martha? (She pulls off her shawl, flings it across a couch and seats herself.)

Martha (lays the duster down and sits): Oh, fine, Judith! I'm so happy that you came over. I haven't been able to get our discussion of yesterday out of my mind. Judith — this Man — all of these miracles — *do* you think that He is the Messiah?

Judith: Martha, I am convinced of it! Why, just this morning Sarah came over and told me of her trip to Bethany. Martha — Sarah *saw* and *talked with* Lazarus, the brother of Mary. It is true! Jesus raised Lazarus from the dead!

Martha: Does Lazarus believe Him to be the Messiah?

Judith: He is definite! And he says that to be near Jesus and to watch His spirit and to listen to His words is the most blessed experience one can receive! There is a transcendent joy and peace that surrounds Him at all times.

Martha: Oh, Judith, isn't it wonderful? The Messiah, for whom we have so long prayed and waited is actually here with us in fulfillment of the Scriptures — and in answer to our prayers.

(There is a pause — while both women sit lost in wonder and meditation. Suddenly from offstage comes a cry. They both look up, startled.)

Deborah (offstage): Mommy! Mommy! Please come quickly!

(Martha jumps to her feet and runs offstage. Judith follows to the left exit but does not leave the stage. There is the sound of excited conversation unintelligible to the audience. Martha and Deborah enter with Martha gently leading Deborah.)

Judith: Deborah, what is it?

Martha: Oh, Deborah, what a scare you did give me! I was so frightened. (She turns to Judith.) I am always hesitant to leave Deborah outside even if she is with her playmates. (She sits and pulls Deborah beside her, smoothing the little girl's hair.) But it's all right now, Deborah. Now (in a little slower manner) explain to Mommy what you are so excited about.

Deborah (eagerly turning her face up to the Martha's, the words tumbling from her lips in a rush of excited and wistful hope): Mommy, my friends say that Jesus is coming this way and that He should be in our city in only a little while. Mommy—oh! Mommy!—Janna said that—that probably—probably—this Jesus could—Mommy! this Jesus could make me see!

(Martha's hand comes up to her throat and her face is one of suffering compassion.)

Martha: Oh, honey!

Deborah: Really, Mommy! Janna said that Jesus raised Lazarus from the dead — so surely He could make my eyes to see! Don't you think so, Aunt Judith?

(Judith comes and kneels by Deborah. She searches Martha's face.)

Deborah: Don't you, Aunt Judith? You believe Jesus could make me see, don't you?

Judith (takes Deborah's hands into her own): Yes, darling, I do!

Martha: Judith!

Judith: Martha, just a moment ago you were sitting here revelling in the wonder of the truth that Jesus is the Christ, our promised Messiah! If that is true — doesn't He have the power to make our little Deborah to see?

(Martha drops her head.)

Judith: Why, Martha, you remember Bartimaeus? He could not see — but Christ gave him back his sight.

Martha (looks up hopefully, searching Judith's face): Do you *really* think there is hope, Judith?

Deborah: Of course there is, Mommy! Janna said that — that Jesus said that He loved everyone — and — and if He loves everyone — then that means that He loves me! And — and — He will make me see, Mommy! Of course, He will! Won't you take me to Him? Won't you — oh! Mommy! — won't you?

(Martha looks at Deborah in perplexity.)

Judith: I'll go with you!

Deborah: Mommy, He will be here soon! Aunt Judith will go! Won't you take me to Jesus? Won't you, Mommy? Jesus will make me see!

Martha (smiles softly): All right, Deborah. I will take you to Jesus!

Judith (stands, smiling): And I will go also. I will rush home and tidy up a bit and then I will be back and we shall go.

(She stoops and kisses Deborah's head; picks up her shawl and exits.)

Deborah: Good! I will get to see Jesus—really, Mommy, I will get to *see* Jesus!

Martha: Darling!

(Martha picks up the brush and begins to brush Deborah's hair.)

Deborah: Mommy, I am *so* happy!

(Barabbas enters with a scowl on his face.)

Martha: Barabbas! You're home early!

Barabbas (growling tone): I should have been later! (He throws a few coins on the table.) I certainly should have waited for the next traveler! (He gestures disdainfully toward the coins.) That is all the man had on him — completely all! I wrung his neck for trying to look like a rich man and being nothing but a pauper! (He spits out the words) A pauper!

Martha: Oh, Barabbas!

Barabbas: I taught him to dress like something he isn't! (He turns toward Deborah and his whole manner changes. He smiles.) And how is my little girl? Didn't I hear you say that you were happy? That is the way Daddy wants his girl to be!

(He takes both her hands in his and kneels, looking in her face.)

Deborah: Daddy, I am happy! Mommy and Aunt Judith are taking me to see Jesus! He is going to make me see!

(Barabbas rises, frowning and glaring at Martha. Martha stands and meets his gaze steadily.)

11

Martha: It is true, Barabbas. We are going to see the Messiah. He should be arriving in our city about now. He raised Lazarus of Bethany from the dead! He healed blind Bartimaeus! He can heal our Deborah!

Barabbas: Are you crazy? Why, you aren't setting foot outside of this house to go to hear or to see that imposter. Why—why, how could you think of such a thing? How could you allow Deborah to get such crazy ideas into her head? How could you? (He turns to Deborah) Baby ——

Deborah: No, Daddy, we are going to see Jesus. Daddy — don't you want me to see again?

Barabbas (pleading): Of course, honey—but it's impossible! Don't you see, Deborah, you have been blind since you were a baby — and — and there is no cure! Daddy has already tried every doctor who knows anything about blindness. This — this man can't ——

Deborah: He is the Messiah, Daddy. He is the promised Son of God!

(There is a knock at the door.)

Martha: That is Judith. She is going to go with us to see Jesus. Good-by, Barabbas. There is food on the table. Come, Deborah!

Barabbas: But, Martha ——

(Martha and Deborah exit. Barabbas stands looking after them in bewilderment. Deborah runs back onstage and throws her arms about his neck.)

Deborah: 'By, Daddy! I'll *see* you when I come back!

(She runs from the room. He stands a moment, staring after her and then slowly he falls to his knees and his head drops into his hands. After a few moments, the groans slip between his lips forming an agonized prayer.)

Barabbas: My God! My God!

(Curtain)

Scene II

(The scene opens upon an empty stage. After a moment, Martha enters, carrying an armful of flowers which she places in a vase and stands arranging them. She hums a little tune as she works. There comes the sound of running feet offstage and then Deborah runs into the room.)

Deborah: Oh, Mother, what beautiful flowers! Where did you find them? Mother, isn't the world beautiful? Janna and I have been running over all of the hills about the city and I can't take in all of the beauty that I've missed for so long! (She throws her arms joyfully about Martha.) Isn't Jesus wonderful to heal me? Oh, Mommy, isn't Jesus wonderful?

Martha: Yes, darling, He is so good and so kind! When He looked at you that day, there was so much tenderness and love that encircled you — that I knew your eyes could not remain blinded to its warmth. At that moment, I could feel my entire being tingling with a deep, strong surge of purity and sweetness which I had never known before.

Deborah: Mommy, I just can't wait for Daddy to come home and to see me — and for me to *see* him! Oh, I just can't wait!

(Martha frowns and studies Deborah a moment and then, with sudden resolution, speaks.)

Martha: Deborah, honey — you know when we came home from seeing Jesus, that Daddy was gone?

Deborah: Yes — and I'll be so happy when he returns!

Martha: Darling, there is something that I must tell you. Come and sit with me.

(They sit together.)

Deborah: Why, Mommy, what is the matter? What could possibly make you unhappy *now?* You are unhappy, aren't you?

Martha: Deborah, when we returned from seeing Jesus that day, I found a note which your daddy had left for me. It — it stated that Roman soldiers had come while we were gone — and — and they were taking your daddy to prison. Darling — I just couldn't tell you then. I couldn't cast a shadow over your happiness!

Deborah: But, Mommy, he will come back home again, won't he?

Martha (sadly): Sweetheart, your father is a murderer and a robber. All of these lovely things (she gestures about the stage) that he has given to us have come through force. I have begged and pleaded with him to give up that bad life and to begin again — but he would never listen. You must understand, Deborah. It is the only life he has ever known. His parents were both thieves. (She bursts into tears.) Oh, Deborah!

(Deborah sits for a moment as if in thought and then puts her arms about her mother.)

Deborah: Mommy, isn't the Feast of the Passover coming soon? Don't they always release a prisoner at that time?

Martha (nods her head and wipes her eyes): Yes, darling, but it is a prisoner whom the people choose to release. Your father is the most hated and feared man of our generation. He would never be chosen to be released. Never!

Deborah (thinking): The doctors said that I would never see! Never! But Jesus changed all of that! Jesus can set Daddy free!

Martha: Deborah!

Deborah: Come, Mommy, let us pray.

(She falls to her knees and, after a moment, Martha kneels.)

Deborah: Lord Jesus, You made my eyes to see. My Mommy said that You made her sweet and pure. Now I ask that You set my daddy free. (There is a pause.) Thank You, Jesus. Thank You. Amen.

(They get to their feet. Deborah points to the flower arrangement.)

Deborah: You had better make a prettier arrangement than that! You know, I can be a critic now! (She smiles.) And Daddy will be here soon!

(Deborah exits. Martha stands looking after her and then slowly turns and begins the arrangement of the flowers.)

(Suddenly the lights are turned down.)

Martha: It looks like a storm is coming.

Deborah (enters): Mommy, the sky is awfully black.

Martha: I know, dear. A storm must be coming. (She frowns.) It certainly has come up fast. You had better stay in the house now.

(Martha is working with the flowers; Deborah stands looking out of a window. After a moment, Barabbas enters quietly and stands in the doorway.)

Deborah (turns, sees him, and runs joyfully to him): Daddy! Daddy! I *see* you! I *see* you!

Barabbas (takes her hands): Is it really true?

Deborah: Yes, Daddy! It is really true! I *see* you! My prayers are *all* answered! Jesus gave me my eyesight! Jesus gave me my daddy back again — just like I prayed!

(Barabbas shows his complete humility and gratitude in his facial expression which he raises toward heaven.)

Barabbas: Jesus — Jesus — Yes, truly, He is the Son of God! He gave back eyesight! He gave joy and love! And — and — at this moment, He is hanging upon *my* cross — suffering for *my* sins — dying in *my* place!

(Curtain)

Hidden Voice: "Greater love hath no man than this, that a man lay down his life for his friends" (John 15:13).

Leader, stress the fact that for each of us, as for Barabbas, Jesus took *our* cross, suffered for *our* sin — and died in *our* place that we might have life everlasting.

DAY OF DECISION

Characters

John: the beloved disciple
Judas: the betrayer
Caiaphas: the high priest
Annas: his father-in-law
Reader

Setting

The setting for the first scene is on a barren stage. It would be well to have backdrops depicting a solitary valley, but if this is not feasible, an empty stage will do. The second scene is on the steps of the hall of Pilate. If backdrops are available, this should be a large, magnificent building with huge columns and pillars. This should take place in front of the steps leading up to the building. If backdrops are not accessible, have lanterns placed about upon large, upright beams. Steps should be arranged leading up to a doorway in center of stage.

Costuming

John should be dressed plainly but neatly. Judas should be gaunt, unkempt. His tunic should be torn and old, his hair and beard long and uncared for. Annas and Caiaphas should be dressed as richly and lavishly as possible. Each item of costuming should indicate great wealth. They should have long, well-groomed beards.

Properties

A money bag, pieces of silver (more than thirty), a rough stick and a spotlight will be needed for the skit.

Skit

Scene I

(Judas and John walk on stage together. There is an air of seriousness about them. John shows concern for his friend. Judas is deep in thought.)

Judas: John . . . God protects Jesus, doesn't He? He would never allow anything to harm Him!

John: Judas! What a thing to ask! God doesn't alter His laws for anyone — not even for Jesus!

Judas (annoyed): Oh!

John: Judas! Judas! What is it? Something has come over you lately. What is it, Judas?

Judas: Why — why there's nothing, John. Everything is fine — just fine!

John: That isn't true, Judas. Something is weighing on your mind. Tell me, Judas. What is wrong?

Judas: Wrong? (He laughs sardonically.) What could be wrong? I am continually in the presence of the Son of God. What could possibly be wrong in my life?

John (sadly): Judas, even in the best climate, one can go wrong. Don't you see that even if you are in His presence now — but are turning ever so slightly away—you can make the wrong choice?

Judas (quickly): Choice?—what choice could be facing me, John?

15

John: I — I'm not certain, Judas. But I do know that you are in a day of decision. And I am certain that it all comes down to the eternal choice that you must make between the world and God. Judas, you will have to make a decision as to whether you care more for the things you can grasp and hold in your hands — or for the lofty ideals and staunch loyalty to Christ.

Judas: How you do talk! Now be good — won't you? and run along and let me think?

John: Judas, don't close your eyes to the truth. You can refuse to see until you become blind to the enormity of sin.

Judas (irritated): Oh, go on — won't you?

(John stands, looking sadly at Judas for a moment. Judas drops his eyes and shifts uneasily.)

John: All right, Judas, I'll go.

(John exits. Judas watches him go, obvious bewilderment and perplexity on his face. After a moment, he steps forward, and holds out his hand pleadingly.)

Judas: John —— (He stops and drops his hand.) No, it is better this way. I must make the choice!

(Judas paces the stage in a tumult of inner emotions. Even at this point, his acting is very important and he should show to the audience the storm going on within him.)

(Caiaphas and Annas enter.)

Caiaphas: Ah! Here's our man! Right on time in the appointed place! You are a man of your word, Judas Iscariot! I do hope that we can complete the bargain immediately.

(Judas looks at him, bitterly worried.)

Caiaphas: Surely, you are not going to let us down now! You wouldn't do that?

Judas (to himself): I don't know.

(Caiaphas looks quickly at Annas. Annas steps forward.)

Caiaphas: You aren't a man to go back on your word!

Judas (flaring with anger): I haven't given my word — yet!

Annas: But you will?

Judas: I don't know. I haven't decided.

Caiaphas (urgently): Then you must decide — now — quickly!

Judas: The decision is mine!

(There is a pause while Caiaphas and Annas study Judas.)

Annas (softly, persuasively): Judas, if you will help us to capture this Jesus, you will be granting a great blessing to our entire nation. Why, He only stirs up the people and causes trouble! And for your doing us — and the nation — this service, we are prepared to pay you!

Caiaphas: Yes, we will pay you handsomely. (He pulls out a pouch and counts out thirty pieces of silver. Judas watches him greedily. Caiaphas holds the money out before Judas. In his other hand, he leaves the bag open, revealing more coins.)

Annas: And not only with money will we pay you, but our entire nation will give to you honor and homage because you have been so patriotic as to bring about the arrest of this troubler of our nation. Everywhere you go, people will bow in salutations and you will gain the friendship of the rich and powerful men of our times. (He steps closer, bringing this next argument in with emphasis.) Why — you could even be given a chief seat in the synagogue as a result of your assistance to us!

(Judas stands a moment, frowning in concentration, and then turns and walks toward the exit. He pauses a moment, then stoops, picks up a small stick that lies on the stage and squeezes it in his hands. Caiaphas and Annas stand watching him. Then Caiaphas steps closer to him, holding out the money.)

Caiaphas: Just lead us to this man — and this money is all yours! Look at your tunic. It is torn. You do need a new one, don't you, Judas? With this money, you will be wealthy. You can dress the way all honorable men dress.

Annas: And you will be one of those honorable men, Judas, if you assist your country in this manner!

Caiaphas: Man, don't just stand there! It is such a simple thing to do! And this money — all of it — will be yours!

(Judas looks at the money and then away. He steps closer to the front of the stage, still deep in thought. He speaks to himself.)

Judas. Decision — ah yes, John — decision! Which choice, after all, will bring to me the largest gain? Shall I join the ranks with these scheming calculating priests who offer me money for the arrest of the One who has stirred up all Israel with His teachings of goodness and love — (he shakes his head in frustration) — but He will not declare Himself to be king! (He pauses.) Shall I join ranks with these men — or shall I give my unswerving loyalty to Christ?

Caiaphas: That would be very foolish to give your loyalty to Christ now, wouldn't it? He will be taken sooner or later. Why not allow it to be at your gain? You even admit that He has stirred up all Israel!

Judas: What shall I do?

(He must show the agony of torment going on within his soul.)

Caiaphas: Take the money, Judas. You will be wealthy! Think of yourself, man! Not of that lowly Nazarene!

Judas: Yes, this is the choice that I must make! Do I choose to live for myself — or for Christ?

Annas (coming to Judas): A man cannot be responsible for another, Judas. You need to learn to think of yourself and what you

17

would enjoy. You would enjoy honor, prestige, a seat in the synagogue, friendship with the elite, and wealth, wouldn't you?

Judas (thinking quickly): And Christ really wouldn't be harmed! God would protect Him! I've seen Him work miracles greater than escaping from their hands. (He frowns.) John said that God would not alter His laws — not even for Christ! (He brings his head up. He is coming close to a decision.) But John was wrong! Christ wouldn't be harmed! And I would have the money!

Annas: Of course, you would have the money! Come now! Let us make the transaction. Come on, take the money — and we will meet you tonight behind the temple just as it gets dark.

(Judas clenches the stick in one hand and pulls his beard with the other. His acting here is of utmost importance. He must portray an inner struggle for destiny. Finally, in a moment of desperate decision, he reaches out, grabs the coins from the hand of Caiaphas.)

Judas: All right! All right! I will meet you behind the temple when it becomes dark!

(He turns and walks swiftly from the stage. Caiaphas and Annas look at each other, smiling in triumph.)

SCENE II

(Caiaphas and Annas walk onto stage.)

Caiaphas (exhilarated): I am certain that Pilate will grant His crucifixion. I have the guarantee from Crimeon that the mob will continue their demands of crucifixion regardless of Pilate's tricks to sway them another way!

Annas (thoughtfully): I wonder why Pilate is trying so hard to save Him?

Caiaphas: Does it matter? The only thing that matters is that we are now rid of this Jesus! I am certain that He will be condemned.

(Judas rushes onto the stage. His face is filled with agony and horror. His right hand clutches the neck of the empty money sack and he holds the thirty coins in his outstretched left hand. He rushes up to the two men, thrusting the money before their faces.)

Judas: He is going to be condemned! I have betrayed innocent blood! I have sinned! I have sinned!

(Annas looks at him with scorn and loathing. Caiaphas holds up his hand in a self-righteous gesture that shows complete unconcern.)

Caiaphas (icily): What is that to us? See thou to that!

Judas (hysterically): You tempted me with your cheap bait and I thought that I could get away with it! You lied and I believed you! I have sinned! I have sinned! I have betrayed innocent blood!

(Caiaphas and Annas look at him contemptuously and then turn away and exit.)

Judas: I have sinned! I have sinned!

(He looks at the coins in his hand with horror and loathing. He flings them to the steps.)

Judas: And it can't be undone! I am lost! — lost forever! Lost — without Christ — without hope — I am lost!

(He runs off stage.)

(The lights are turned down and a spotlight is placed upon the scattered coins upon the empty steps.)

Reader (from backstage. Much depends upon his expression and vocal quality here.): Judas Iscariot — one of the chosen twelve — one whom Jesus loved dearly. He walked and talked with the Master in intimate relationship. But in spite of his every advantage, he allowed sin to blind his eyes. Judas didn't know that he was going to put Jesus to death. He was only going to make extra money. He didn't know what he was doing because he was blinded by sin.

Sin always does that. Sin is appealing like red wine sparkling in a glass in temptation — after the sin has been committed, it bites and destroys like a serpent. Sin makes one do what can never be undone. Sin offers the attractive, enticing things first; then come the bitter dregs.

In the life of Judas, the coins were wonderful, jingling about in his pocket. But they turned into spears of heartbreak. And — in agony, Judas went to the priests who had tempted him and they turned away in sublime unconcern for this broken man.

Sin acts like that. It will offer you a price — and then it's through with you. You will be left with only the broken pieces of the lovely dreams that were yours — and the life which you could have known. Sin lies, cheats, destroys and damns!

(Leader, take over the service for the invitation.)

THE CHOICE

Characters

Zacchaeus: a tax collector (choose actor with care; much depends upon his ability to handled the lines)

Ariah: a disgruntled old man

Benjamin: a friend of Zacchaeus

Setting

Both scenes should be depicted in the office of Zacchaeus. The office should be arranged and furnished as lavishly as possible.

Costuming

Zacchaeus and Benjamin should be richly dressed in the style of Biblical times. They should have large, conspicuous rings on their fingers. Ariah should be dressed in faded but neat clothing. He wears no jewelry.

Properties

There should be some large books for Zacchaeus' desk, a notebook, ink and quill with which he writes; a money box inside his desk with coins (silvery). There should be a money bag with silvery coins for Ariah, and a sign stating: "Zacchaeus: Collector of Taxes of Jericho," should be placed on the front of his desk. A sheaf of papers representing the "jail certifications" should also be accessible.

Skit

SCENE I

(Zacchaeus is sitting at his desk. He is writing. He looks up sourly, shakes his quill a few times, writes again, throws the quill down in anger, and leans back in his chair.

Zacchaeus: I wish I could find a quill somewhere that would write for longer than three seconds at a time! My ulcers are acting up today and I feel in a rotten mood! Of course — that is my usual state of mind! I don't know why I don't get used to it!

(He sits for a moment with eyes closed. Then, with determination, he sits up, takes the quill in hand, dips in ink, and begins to write again.)

(Ariah enters. Zacchaeus lays down the quill and smiles.)

Zacchaeus: Good day, Ariah. What can I do for you?

Ariah (sourly): If I were you, I would turn on the smile also! You know that it is time for you to figure my tax again — which you will do by multiplying the just amount by five!

Zacchaeus: Now, Ariah, don't say such hard things! You know that we tax collectors are very honest in our dealings!

Ariah: Rubbish! You don't understand the meaning of the word "honesty!" You think that it only means that you should be concerned with yourself — which you do all of the time in the most elaborate style!

Zacchaeus: Thank you very much, Ariah. I am glad that you appreciate my style. And now about this tax ——

Ariah: Yes, let's do hurry. You can hardly wait to get your hands on the little remaining money that I have left after your last taxing expedition!

Zacchaeus: Ah, yes — I am glad that you mentioned our last

20

taxing expedition for that brings to my mind the fact that I was out walking in your vineyard the other day.

Ariah (heatedly): And what were you doing in my vineyard?

Zacchaeus: Calm down, Ariah, just calm down! I wouldn't have been in your vineyard, had I known that it was yours, for I would not have felt welcome! But, you see, you reported to me last time that you had only one vineyard which was on the front acreage of your land. I just happened to be riding around the back portion of your land the other day and found this luscious vineyard. Now, of course, I knew that it was not your vineyard or you would have reported it, so I talked with the servants to discover who had leased it from you!

Ariah: Dog!

Zacchaeus: And I discovered that you, yourself, had a vineyard on the back portion of your land! And it was not reported!

Ariah: Zacchaeus, you know that those plants are still very young. They have never borne fruit. Why should I report something that I don't have?

Zacchaeus: But, wasn't the vineyard under cultivation the last time you reported for taxation?

Ariah: Well — yes — but it wasn't bearing! You were there! You know yourself that it has never borne any fruit!

Zacchaeus: But it was under cultivation — so I will have to charge you for back tax this time!

Ariah: Back tax no such thing! Zacchaeus, you know that that vineyard has given me no income even yet — and certainly not before! I didn't report its cultivation because I thought ——

Zacchaeus (holding up his hand): That is where you made your mistake, Ariah! *You* thought! It doesn't matter what you think! It is what I think!

Ariah (bitterly): And what would be to your greater gain! You would have charged me for it under cultivation as much as if it were a full producing vineyard!

Zacchaeus: You do know me well, don't you, Ariah? Now, about your tax, let's see! (He pulls out a book and studies it for a moment.)

Ariah: Do have mercy just this once, Zacchaeus! My little ——

Zacchaeus: Don't try to tell me your sob story, Ariah! I am interested only in your tax. Now, that will be eighty pieces of silver!

Ariah (taken back): Eighty pieces — oh, Zacchaeus! I knew that you were a hard man — but never did I dream this — Zacchaeus, you know that my vineyard — even counting the back portion is only a very tiny one. It does not yield much at best! Zacchaeus—I can't——

Zacchaeus: You can either pay or go to jail! Ariah, which shall it be? I have jail certifications right here.

(Zacchaeus pulls out a sheaf of papers. Ariah looks at him pleadingly.)

Ariah: Zacchaeus — this once — please — I must have money for my little girl ——

Zacchaeus (hard): Which shall it be, Ariah? Eighty pieces of silver — or jail?

(Ariah looks at Zacchaeus pleadingly for a moment, turns away with bowed head and finally sighs deeply and pulls the money bag from his pocket. He empties its contents before Zacchaeus and walks heavily from the room. Zacchaeus watches him go, then laughs, places the coins in the money box in the desk drawer. He leans back in the chair, contented.)

Zacchaeus: I'll teach him to try to play tricks on Zacchaeus! Eighty pieces of silver! (He laughs uproariously.)

(Benjamin enters.)

Benjamin: Good day, Zacchaeus. What is so funny?

Zacchaeus: Oh, good day, Benjamin. Do have a seat. Old Ariah was just here and I charged him for his tax. Get this Benjamin — eighty pieces of silver!

Benjamin: Eighty pieces of silver! For his tiny vineyard, Zacchaeus?

Zacchaeus: He has enlarged his tiny vineyard and did not tell of his intent last time — so I made up for his oversight!

Benjamin: I should say that you did make up for it quite adequately!

Zacchaeus: It is good to see you, Benjamin. What has brought you to Jericho?

Benjamin: Zacchaeus, I wanted to talk with you.

Zacchaeus (amazed): You came all the way here just to talk with me?

Benjamin: Yes. You have been my friend since boyhood and some things have been happening recently—that, well—I wanted to talk with you. Are you free?

Zacchaeus: I have some more paper work to complete but it is not pressing. Tell me, what is so important that it brought you this long way to see me?

Benjamin: Zacchaeus, have you ever seen Jesus of Nazareth?

Zacchaeus (surprised): Why, no! Why do you ask?

Benjamin: I heard Him speak the other day. As I listened, my heart burned within me. My cheeks flushed with shame and remorse.

Zacchaeus: Shame and remorse?

Benjamin: Shame for the way I have cheated people in the tax office in Bethany — and remorse for having made the wrong decision!

Zacchaeus: Benjamin, you mustn't be like that! We talked it all over before we decided to enter the tax business. It was either popularity or wealth. And if we chose one, we could not expect the other.

Benjamin: I know. We made our choice, understanding its cost. But I felt, as I listened to Christ speak, that we had made the wrong decision. For the first time in many years, I felt sick, helpless, and in need of Someone who cared! When Jesus had finished speaking, He turned away from the group for a moment. For some unexplained reason, I stepped closer to Him. He turned — and finding me there — looked long into my eyes and — and then He said: "Behold, I stand at the door and knock: if any man hear My voice and open the door, I will come in to Him, and will sup with him and he with Me."

Zacchaeus: Of course, He didn't mean that, Benjamin. He knew that you were a tax collector, didn't He?

Benjamin (nods): He knew, Zacchaeus. And He loved me anyway.

Zacchaeus: And this Christ — He would love me?

Benjamin: More than you can possibly begin to understand — He would love you, Zacchaeus. It is something that goes beyond the grasp of our little minds! His love is infinite, compassionate, divine. Zacchaeus, you must promise me that you will go to hear Him when He comes to Jericho!

Zacchaeus (thoughtfully): Yes, Benjamin, I will go to hear Him when He comes.

Benjamin: And — you will open your heart to Him?

Zacchaeus: We'll see! We'll see!

(Curtain)

SCENE II

(Zacchaeus is seated at his desk, writing. He hums a happy tune as he works. Ariah enters. He stands watching Zacchaeus a moment, studying him intently, listening to his song.)

Ariah: Good day, Zacchaeus.

Zacchaeus: And good day to you, Ariah!

(He smiles warmly, gets to his feet and goes to Ariah. He places his arm about Ariah's shoulders.)

Zacchaeus: Won't you have a seat? It is a wonderful day, isn't it?

Ariah (hesitantly): Yes, it is a wonderful day, Zacchaeus — in fact, a most unbelievable day!

Zacchaeus: Ariah, did you see Jesus when He was here? Did you get to listen to Him talk? Did you get to understand His great spirit of love?

Ariah: Uh — no — I didn't, Zacchaeus. But I heard that you did!

Zacchaeus: Indeed I did, and the greatest thing in the world came into my life! Since I know Jesus Christ, my whole attitude toward life — and property — has changed completely. It's all because He dwells now within my heart. And Ariah, I am filled with a joy and a peace that I never knew could exist in this world.

(There is a pause while Zacchaeus is, for a moment, lost in happy thought. Ariah watches him in perplexity.)

Zacchaeus: I'm sorry, Ariah! It's just that it is all so new — and so completely marvelous! Now, the first thing I want to say to you is that I am sorry for cheating you! I was very wrong — blinded by sin! And I want to restore all that I took from you fourfold!

Ariah: But ——

Zacchaeus: No, I want to do it — with interest for my wrongdoing!

(Zacchaeus opens a drawer and counts out a heap of coins which he gives to Ariah. Ariah watches him, dumfounded.)

Zacchæus: Now, that takes care of the debt. You were trying to tell me something about your little girl the other day. What is wrong? Can I help?

Ariah: Well, my little girl has been ill for a long time. We thought that she was going to die. But — my wife took her to see Jesus!

Zacchaeus: I see! And, of course, He made her whole!

(Ariah nods.)

Zacchaeus: Isn't it wonderful? He can make bodies whole — and even greater — He can make our spirits whole! Can I tell you about it?

Ariah: Yes, please!

Zacchaeus: Well, my friend, Benjamin, came to me several days ago and urged me not to miss seeing Jesus when He came to Jericho. I promised that I wouldn't. As soon as I heard that He was in town, I closed up the office and, hurriedly, went to the place where He was supposed to be! A huge crowd was about Him — and since I am smaller than most people — and could hardly expect anyone to show me a favor — I could not even get a glimpse of Him. So, on a sudden inspiration, I ran ahead of the crowd to that tall sycamore tree that stands by the main road. I climbed up and made me a good seat on one of the low-hanging branches. I could see Him then, in the distance, and my heart pounded within me! I watched Him come nearer and nearer. I was leaning from the tree to catch a glimpse of His face as He passed beneath me. But as He came up, He stopped. Then He looked up at me — and smiled! He said: "Zacchaeus, make haste and come down. You must give me a home today." I sat there looking at Him, dumfounded.

In that moment, my own destiny hung in the balance and He, with all of His divine love, patiently waited upon my human reluctance. At that instant, I had come face to face with the perpetual issue between heaven and earth — the greatest issue of life — *Choice!* I faced the challenge of Christ to all mankind. I saw in His eyes the persistent appeal of His love to my lethargy and indifference. He gave to me in that moment a call for decision! — decision between right and wrong — between earthly values and things eternal — decision between heaven and hell!

Ariah, divine love stood under that sycamore tree and waited with outstretched hands for me to allow Him to make His home in my heart. And when I slipped out of that tree, something wonderful happened! Death fell away! Life became mine! Old things passed away; all things became new!

Ariah, He stands today offering His love to you! Won't you let Him in?

(Ariah slips to his knees in consecration.)

(Curtain)

Leader: Jesus, with divine love, entered the heart of Zacchaeus and something wonderful happened. He was ready and waiting to enter the heart of Ariah. And He longs to fill your heart just now with His love so that you, too, can understand that "something wonderful" which happens when Christ Jesus comes to dwell within a life. When you accept Him, He blesses each phase of your life, enhances each activity, illuminates each duty, and fills daily living with joy unspeakable and full of glory!

As in the life of Zacchaeus, He comes to your heart this night and, in this moment, your destiny hangs in the balance as He, with all of His divine love, patiently waits upon your human reluctance. In this instant, you are face to face with the perpetual issue between heaven and earth — the greatest issue of life *Choice!* You face the challenge of Christ to all mankind — the persistent appeal of His love to your lethargy and indifference. In this moment, He is asking for decision — decision between right and wrong — between earthly values and things eternal — decision between heaven and hell!

Christ is now standing at your heart's door with outstretched hands seeking admittance. Won't you let Him come in?

Invitation.

SELLOUT

Characters

Jacob: a clean-cut young man who enjoys cooking
Esau: Jacob's brother
Rebecca: the mother of Jacob and Esau
Isaac: their father

Setting

If backdrops are available, a wooded area should be used. In Scene I there should be a tent at the side of the stage. Scene II is presented in the woods and there should be as much wooded scenery place about the stage as possible. Large branches of trees may be placed upright to resemble trees by placing them in a Christmas tree stand and covering up that portion with grass and artificial flowers. In the center of the stage there should be a place for cooking.

Costuming

Jacob is dressed neatly in a tunic and belt. His hair is neatly arranged and in place. Esau is carelessly dressed with his tunic tied over only one shoulder. He wears a water pouch tied about his waist. Rebecca is dressed in Biblical style and wears her hair in braids.

Properties

A "fire" will be necessary for the center of the stage. Chopped wood should be arranged as for a fireplace. It should be blacked and smoked. The fire can be imitated by placing red cellophane "flames" over the wood and about the cooking vessel. A light bulb placed in the wood to shine through the cellophane makes this more realistic. The cooking vessel can be an old fashioned black washpot or it may be arranged with a frame made over the fire and a large cooking vessel hanging by a wire over the fire. A large spoon, a bowl, a wooden spoon, a twig on the ground and "pottage" for the cooking vessel should be available. Esau should have a bow and arrows slung over his shoulder.

Skit

SCENE I

(Jacob is sitting cross-legged by the fire, looking dreamily into space. Esau enters, looks at him askance.)

Esau: What are you doing?

Jacob (jumps a little): Oh — just thinking, Esau.

Esau: Thinking! About what?

Jacob (shrugs): Things! Going hunting?

Esau: Yeah, I'm going to see what I can find. (He pats his bow gently.) Me and this little item are the terror of the forest! (He laughs.)

Jacob: Esau! I don't see how you stand it!

Esau: You ought to try it sometime. You might discover what a wonderful sport it is — as well as mighty fine tasting when the catch has been cooked!

Jacob: I'll let you do the hunting; I'll do the cooking, thank you.

Esau: You don't know what you're missing!

Jacob: Then, please allow me to remain in my ignorance!

Esau: Have it your way! (He gestures toward the fire.) Cooking?

Jacob (laughs ruefully): I'm trying. It's beginning to bubble! I thought it would never get hot. That fire was stubborn to get started. How long will you be gone?

Esau: Oh, three or four days, I guess. And I'd better get started! So long, brother!

Jacob: Good-by, Esau!

(Esau exits. Jacob watches him go, then leans forward, picks up the spoon and stirs the "pottage." He picks up a spoonful and smells of it. He wrinkles his nose.)

Jacob: It hasn't even started!

(Rebecca enters.)

Rebecca: Good morning, Jacob. Are you alone? I thought I heard voices.

Jacob: Yes, my dear brother, Esau, was here a minute ago giving me a running commentary on the thrills of hunting! I was quite relieved when he decided to go prove those thrills to himself.

Rebecca: For shame, Jacob. You shouldn't talk that way about your brother.

Jacob: Oh, Mother! You know the depth of brotherly love that exists between Esau and me!

Rebecca: Well, I don't like to be reminded!

Jacob (hesitates): Mother! I want to ask you something! What, exactly, is this birthright that is to be given to Esau because he is the oldest child?

Rebecca (sits): Jacob, I've explained that to you before. The firstborn son has a great responsibility in the family. He is entitled to what we call the "birthright." He will serve as the priest and the judge of our family.

Jacob: At the same time?

Rebecca: Yes. As the firstborn, Esau will become the chief of the Hebrew tribe after the death of your father, and in this manner he will be the heir to the covenant which was made by God with Abraham.

Jacob: I see. It's pretty important, isn't it? Heir to a covenant with God!

Rebecca: Yes, it is important, Jacob. Most important!

Jacob: And it goes to Esau!

(Rebecca sighs and arises.)

Rebecca: Yes, Jacob, it goes to Esau.

Isaac (offstage): Rebecca! Rebecca! Where are you?

Rebecca: Oh, that is your father. I must go to him. Take good care of your pottage, Jacob!

(She pauses, picks up the spoon, and stirs.)

Isaac (offstage): Rebecca! Rebecca!

Rebecca: I'm coming, dear!

(She smells of a spoonful of the soup. She lays the spoon down.)

Rebecca: It has hopes, Jacob. Yes, it smells delicious. You are becoming quite good at this, you know!

Jacob (sourly): It's nice to know that I'm good at something!

Rebecca: Jacob, don't be like that!

Jacob: And how should I be? Excited and exuberant because my older brother will inherit the birthright? He will receive the covenant of God!

Rebecca: Jacob, don't worry about it, dear.

Isaac (offstage): Rebecca!

Rebecca: Oh, I must go! Jacob, promise me that you won't worry about it. All will be well!

Jacob (sarcastically): I'm sure that it will!

Rebecca: Now promise me that you won't worry! Promise!

Jacob: All right, I promise that I won't worry!

Rebecca (pats his head): That's a good boy!

Isaac (offstage): Rebecca! Where are you?

Rebecca: I'm coming! I'm coming!

(Rebecca exits.)

Jacob: I won't worry! What good does that do? For that matter, what good does anything do?

(He rolls over on his stomach and picks up a twig from the stage. He chews on it thoughtfully for a moment.)

Jacob: I wonder — I just wonder — if I could, somehow, take that birthright away from him! I just wonder!

(He is silent a moment, chewing on the twig.)

Jacob: But how? That is the question now — how?

(He chews on the twig thoughtfully and then, still thinking, he sits up, picks up the spoon and stirs the "pottage.")

Jacob: The covenant of God! I want that for my own! I want it at any cost! I must find a way! I simply must find a way!

(He picks up a spoonful of the soup, wiggles his nose appreciatively, and tastes it. A crafty gleam comes into his eyes.)

Jacob: Say — this might be it! It just might be ——

(Curtain)

SCENE II

(Jacob is sitting by the fire with a big spoon in his hand.)

Jacob: Esau has been gone four days now on his hunting expedition and so I came out here to welcome him back to civilization.

28

(He laughs and stirs the "pottage.") He always comes home this way and he should be along any moment. I should imagine that he will be happy about getting out of the forest — and having the opportunity to eat some good hot pottage from my most experienced hand! (He tastes a spoonful of the "pottage.") Umm! Mighty good! Even if I do say so myself, it is mighty, mighty good pottage!

(There is the sound of heavy footsteps offstage. Esau enters.)

Esau: Jacob! What are you doing out here?

Jacob: You seemed to think I might enjoy life in the woods, brother. I thought that I should see for myself!

Esau (sniffing the air hungrily): I smell something — and it smells terrific!

Jacob: Any success with your hunting?

Esau: No — some messenger had been out in the forest to warn all of the animals of the coming of the great hunter! There was nary a living form in sight! Honest! (He laughs ruefully.)

(Esau pulls off his bow and arrow and flings them to the ground. He unties the water pouch from around his waist and drops it to the ground. Jacob stirs the pottage.)

Esau (looking into the cooking vessel): Brother, your cooking is becoming quite a skill!

Jacob: Thank you, Esau. I was just complimenting myself upon my ability!

Esau (drops wearily to the ground): Well now, brother, aren't you going to offer me some of that pottage? I can hardly wait!

Jacob: And just why should I offer you some pottage? I am the one who cooked it while you have been off galavanting around!

Esau: Come now, Jacob! You know you enjoy this kind of thing! Man, I'm starved — positively famished! Serve me quickly else I die!

(Jacob looks at Esau craftily.)

Jacob: Are you really hungry, Esau?

Esau: Really hungry? I am famished! I am not teasing you when I say that I must eat immediately or I will die of starvation! Come now, brother, don't tease with me! Give me food!

(Jacob holds up a spoonful of the "pottage" and waves it under Esau's nose. Esau sniffs hungrily.)

Esau: Cut it out now! Give me a bowl full — not a spoonful — what are you trying to do — kill me with temptation?

(Jacob stirs the pottage thoughtfully.)

Esau (impatiently): Jacob, give me some pottage! I'm famished!

Jacob: I will sell you a bowl of pottage.

Esau: Sell me a bowl? For what?

Jacob: I will sell you a bowl of this pottage — for your birthright!

Esau (incredulously): My birthright?

29

Jacob: That's right! Those are my terms!

Esau: Don't be ridiculous! Jacob, give me something to eat!

Jacob: You heard my proposition. You sell me your birthright for a bowl of pottage. You keep your birthright—I keep my pottage!

Esau: Jacob, really!

Jacob: Really! Which will it be? Your birthright? Or some of this delicious pottage?

(Jacob holds up a spoonful under Esau's nose.)

Esau: Oh, all right! I'm about to die of starvation! What good would the birthright be to me if I were dead?

Jacob: Good thinking, brother! Will you sell me your birthright?

Esau: Yes, all right, I said that I would. Now give me some of that pottage!

(Again Jacob holds up a spoonful of pottage under Esau's nose.)

Jacob: Swear that you will give me your birthright for a bowl of pottage!

Esau: I swear! Jacob — please!

Jacob: Then it's a deal! Pottage coming up, dear brother. Pottage coming right up!

(Jacob spoons up a bowl of pottage and hands it to Esau. Esau grabs the bowl and begins hungrily to eat the pottage. After a few moments, he pauses and looks at Jacob.)

Esau: Jacob, you didn't really mean that, did you? About the birthright, I mean! I really couldn't sell my birthright — just for a measly bowl of pottage!

Jacob: You just did!

Esau: No, Jacob, you don't mean it! Just for a bowl of pottage!

Jacob: A mighty cheap price, I must admit. But it was a deal!

Esau: But Jacob, I can't sell something eternal merely for a passing whim!

Jacob: You did!

(Esau sets the bowl down and arises in obvious agitation.)

Esau: Jacob, you can't do this!

Jacob: I just did! You sold your birthright, brother dear, for a bowl of pottage!

Esau (pacing the stage): But I didn't mean to! I didn't mean to! I just didn't think! I didn't think! Yes, that was my downfall! I just didn't think! I didn't intend to lose my covenant with the Lord. I— I was simply carried away with the desire of the moment! Now it's done! And it can't be undone!

(Esau goes to Jacob.)

Esau: Please, Jacob. I didn't really mean it!

Jacob (laughs): I am so sorry, brother dear, so sorry! But a deal is a deal! You sold your covenant with God for a bowl of pottage!

(Esau turns away.)

Esau: For such a paltry sum, for such a cheap, fleeting desire, I gave up the most important thing in my life. I sold out! And now the decision cannot be revoked. It's too late to think clearly now! It's too late! I sold my covenant with God for a bowl of pottage! I sold out, and now it can never be undone! Sold out!

(Curtain)

Leader: Esau lived only for the present; he did not look beyond his own immediate desires. Esau was completely taken up in the pleasures of satisfying his senses; he cared only for fun on a day-to-day basis. Esau was a foolish spendthrift of the most valuable things in his life. He sold out his covenant with God for a mere bowl of pottage.

Sin would have *you* live only for the present, not look beyond your immediate desires, become absorbed in the pleasures of your senses, care only for fun for the present — and in this way, you, too, will be a spendthrift of the most valuable things in your life! You will sell out your manhood and your womanhood for things as trivial and fleeting as a bowl of pottage. You will sell out your character and your dreams for a flimsy thrill and then you will find yourself a broken, mangled bit of humanity with no hope, no dreams, no relationship with God.

Invitation.

WHOM YE SERVE

Characters

Elisha: successor of Elijah, the prophet
Baasha: his brother
Deborah: his mother

Setting

The setting is in the garden of the home of Elisha's parents. There should be several chairs sitting about the stage and as much greenery and flowers as possible. If backdrops are available, a beautiful scenic view would do well. An old well with a bucket in one corner of the stage would be appropriate.

Costuming

Elisha, Baasha, and Deborah are dressed in neat, moderately wealthy fashion of the Biblical period. Baasha should be attired more youthfully than the other two characters.

Properties

A basket for Baasha's lunch should be available. Soft music could be heard in the background.

Skit

SCENE I

(Baasha comes running onto the empty stage, obviously very excited.)

Baasha: Mother! Mother!

(Deborah comes on stage.)

Deborah: What is it, Baasha?

Baasha: Mother! Mother! The prophet — Elijah — He is here! He is here, Mother!

Deborah: The prophet Elijah, Baasha? Are you certain?

Baasha: Yes — Yes — I'm sure! He said that it was Elijah — the prophet of God, Mother!

Deborah: Who said that it was Elijah, Baasha?

Baasha: The man in the market place. He said that the prophet of God, Elijah, had come! And — and he said that he had come to challenge King Ahab! And, Mother — he said that Elijah was going to destroy Baal! That's what he said, Mother, honest!

Deborah (frowning): Challenge King Ahab — Destroy Baal? I don't understand what you are talking about, Baasha — and I certainly don't understand who told you! Come, sit down and try to collect yourself, dear. Now, tell me what this is all about.

(They sit.)

Baasha: Well, I was in the market place a while ago — getting you some grapes — you know——

Deborah (nods impatiently): Yes, yes!

Baasha: Well, I was in the market place when this messenger of King Ahab came in. Mother, he was dressed in the most splendid clothes! Anyway, he got up on a big stone and called everyone's attention. And then — and then — he said that the prophet of the Lord — Elijah — had come to town and that he had commanded King Ahab to call all the people together on Mount Carmel! Mother, he said that they were going to have a test to prove once and for all whether the Lord is God — or whether we should worship this old stone image, Baal!

Deborah (wonderingly): A test to prove whether the Lord is God!

Baasha: And he said that all of the prophets of Baal would be there to do their stuff — but God only needs one prophet! Doesn't He, Mother? Elijah is enough for God!

(Deborah rises, her eyes shining. Her hands are clasped over her breast. She walks toward front of stage, thinking, with a blissful expression on her face.)

Deborah: At last, it has come! At last! Baal is going to be shown for the stone image he is to all of the people. (She smiles.) And all of the 400 prophets of Baal will not be able to stand against the one prophet of God! Oh — what a glorious sight that will be! Once again, God will reign in Israel! (She turns.) Baasha, you must go to Mount Carmel. I want you to be there when God proves Himself once more!

Baasha (jumps to his feet): Oh, Mother — really — do you honestly mean it? Really? I wanted to go so badly — but I was afraid to ask!

(Deborah pauses and thinks a moment.)

Deborah: It is quite a distance from here ——

Baasha (quickly): Mother, it isn't that far! You've already said that I could go!

(Deborah laughs and rumples his hair.)

Deborah: Don't be so worried, child! I was only thinking that it is quite a distance from here and you will be gone a good while. So I had better fix you a lunch. Is that all right?

Baasha (grins): You know I always vote for food!

Deborah: Well — I must get at it immediately. You should leave just as quickly as possible.

(Deborah starts for right exit and then stops.)

Deborah: Oh — if only Elisha were here to go with you! How much it would mean to your brother if he could be present at this great event when God's power will be made manifest once more. You must remember everything that happens, Baasha, so that you can repeat it all to Elisha.

(Deborah smiles at Baasha and then exits.)

Baasha: Oh, I'll love to tell Elisha all about it! He is always the one telling me about his adventures. Now — I can tell him! He hugs himself delightedly.) I'm going — I'm actually going! The things I will have to tell Elisha.

(He trips about the stage in excitement. Deborah enters carrying basket.)

Deborah: Here is your lunch, Baasha! Now — don't lose it and don't become so excited that you forget to eat! And when you have seen God's power defeat everything false and evil — come home to me, Baasha, and tell me all about it!

(Baasha kisses his mother lightly. He takes the basket.)

Baasha: I will do just that!

(Baasha exits. Deborah stands watching him go. She smiles and turns to face audience.)

Deborah: He is such a good boy. (She bites her lip, thinking.) Elisha is a good boy, too. It's just that — now — in his youth — he is at the crossroads. There are so many temptations confronting him just now—so many confusing issues! There are so many of those his age who choose only to live for self! And Elisha doesn't know which road is best — he just doesn't know!

(She lifts her face heavenward in an attitude of prayer.)

Deborah: God, bless my boy, Elisha. Help him to know that only when You reign supreme in His heart can' his life ever find fulfillment and happiness. Amen.

(Curtain)

SCENE II

(Elisha is sitting in a chair, eating some grapes. Baasha dashes on stage.)

Baasha: Mother! Mother!

(Deborah enters. She runs to Baasha.)

Deborah: Baasha! You're home! Are you all right? Did you not get hungry? Was there enough food for you? Are you terribly tired? Oh, Baasha, dear, tell me — how was it?

(Elisha casts the grapes aside and laughs.)

Elisha: Mother — do you want him to answer all of your questions at once — or one at a time?

Deborah: I'm sorry, Baasha! Do sit down, dear. And tell us what happened.

(Deborah and Baasha sit. His eyes are sparkling with enthusiasm and his narration of the day's events are animated and sincere. Elisha leans forward, listens with interest but remains silent.)

Baasha: Well—when I got up on Mount Carmel, Elijah had just begun to speak. You can tell by looking at him, Mother, that he is a man of God. There is just a — a — well — something about him that makes you know that he is a man of God!

(Deborah nods in understanding.)

Baasha: When he came to finish his speech, Elijah said in that great, big, booming voice of his: "How long are you going to waver between two opinions — between Baal and God? If Baal be your god, worship him; but if the Lord be God, then worship Him."

Nobody said anything and then he told us that he was now ready to prove who was really God!

The prophets of Baal built an altar and placed the sacrifice upon it. Then they began to walk around it, chanting all of the time: "O Baal, hear us! O Baal, hear us! O Baal, hear us!" But — there was no response! They did this all morning, and about noon Elijah began to make fun of them and really tease them!

Finally — about sunset — when nothing had happened at all, Elijah rebuilt the altar with twelve stones to represent the twelve tribes. He prepared the sacrifice — and then, Mother, he did the strangest thing! He had trenches dug all about the altar — and then had the men pour water upon the altar until it was drenched and the trenches were full! Then he raised his face toward heaven and he prayed. He said: "Lord God, let it be known now that You are God and that I, as Your servant, have done this thing at Your command. Hear me, O Lord, hear me that this people may know that You are God and will take You into their hearts!"

And then, Mother — and then! — fire fell from heaven! It burned up the sacrifice and the wood — and it even licked up all of the water in the trench! Then — all of the people were crying and saying over and over: "The Lord He is God! The Lord He is God!"

(Deborah has had her hands clasped in joy and has listened with great happiness and praise. She turns to Elisha.)

Deborah: Oh, Elisha! Elisha! Isn't it wonderful? Isn't it wonderful?

(She pauses. Elisha is sitting with his head in his hands. Deborah goes to him.)

Deborah: Elisha — what is the matter?

(Elisha slowly raises his head. His eyes are troubled.)

Elisha: Mother, I have to understand what all of those people came to understand today! I have to decide if I will allow myself to be my god — live only for my desires and interests — or whether I, too, shall say in my heart: The Lord He is God! And, Mother, if I decide that I shall accept the Lord to be my God, what a difference that will make in my life!

(Deborah sits beside him, her eyes searching his face.)

Elisha: Elijah proved today that there is a God on high! And if I choose to ignore that fact, I can allow myself the luxuries of satisfying all of my physical desires — the luxury of living a life completely dedicated to attaining everything that is most pleasing to me! (He is thinking deeply, understanding the seriousness of the issue.) But, on the other hand, if I accept the fact that I am not my own master, but accept the Lord as my God, I will have to crucify myself — and my physical desires — and surrender completely my will to God's will!

Deborah: But God's will is the only perfect way to live, Elisha! Living in God's will will bring to you the beauty of fulfillment, the music of a life completely attuned to the divine. You can only find happiness and goodness in God's way.

Elisha: But God's way is not the easy way, Mother!

Deborah: Not the easy way, my son — but the good way!

Elisha: So I must decide if I want ease — or goodness!

(Deborah nods.)

Deborah: You must choose, my son. I cannot do it for you!

Elisha: No, Mother, you cannot do it for me! Your faith — my father's faith are not enough. This is a personal issue. Every man has to decide for himself what his destiny will be! I must choose if I, Elisha, want ease — or goodness! I must choose if I will live for myself — or if I will live for God!

(Deborah and Baasha bow their heads in an attitude of prayer. Elisha rises and walks to front of stage.)

Elisha: Elijah said: "How long will ye waver between two opinions?" Which will be my God? Myself — or the Lord?

(The lights darken slowly on the stage. Elisha turns his face upward.)

Elisha: I am not wise enough or strong enough to guide my life! It is foolish to even consider allowing self to be my god.

(The music begins in the background at this time. "Just As I Am," will fit these words. Elisha speaks the words with pathos and depth.)

Elisha: Just as I am, Thine own to be,
Friend of the young, who lovest me,
To consecrate myself to Thee,
O Jesus Christ, I come.*

In the glad morning of my day
My life to give, my vows to pay,
With no reserve and no delay,
With all my heart, I come.

I would live ever in the light,
I would work ever for the right,
I would serve Thee with all my might,
Therefore, to Thee I come.

Just as I am, young, strong, and free,
To be the best that I can be
For truth and righteousness and Thee,
Lord of my life, I come. Amen.

(Elisha bows his head.)
(Curtain)

Leader, take charge of the service, using this hymn as your invitation hymn, if desired.

(* This is the poem written by Marianne Farningham in 1887. For this skit taken from the Old Testament, it would be better to change the words: "O Jesus Christ, I come," to "O Lord, my God, I come.")

REDEEMED

Characters

David: teen-age boy
Karen: teen-age girl
Rita: teen-age girl
Hidden Voice
Soloist

Setting

The first scene takes place underneath a tree. If possible, back-drops indicating a wood nearby and, perhaps, a small brook would be advantageous. Artificial grass covering the stage would lend atmosphere. A tree is important. This can be a large branch from a tree placed upright in a Christmas tree stand and the stand covered with grass and flowers. The second scene is an empty stage on which a draped easel stands bearing the picture *Christ on the Cross* by Rubens. This picture is spotlighted.

Costuming

The three teen-agers are in typical school dress. Rita could be overdone with make-up and jewelry.

Properties

David should be carrying school books in the first scene. An easel, velvet for draping, if desired, picture *Christ on the Cross* by Rubens, and a spotlight will be needed for the second scene. The music to the song: *When I Survey the Wondrous Cross* by Isaac Watts should be available.

Skit

SCENE I

(Rita comes on stage from right exit as David and Karen enter from left exit.)

Rita: Hi, David! How are you?

(She comes up to him, rolling her eyes in teasing fashion. She completely ignores Karen.)

David: Hi, Rita! Karen and I are just leaving school. Are you returning?

Rita (coquettishly): Only long enough to see if I could find a good looking boy to walk me home!

David: I hope you find one! I'm walking Karen home!

(Rita looks at Karen sardonically.)

Rita: Really?

David (flaring): Really!

Rita: Well — you used to have better taste than that, David! Don't you want to walk me home again?

David: Karen and I must go now, Rita. Good-by!

Rita: But I'm not going anywhere!

David: But we are!

(David pushes past her and he and Karen walk over to the tree. Rita stands watching them, chagrined. When they sit underneath the tree, Rita flounces off stage.)

David: Let me apologize for her actions! I'm terribly sorry that happened!

Karen: It's all right, David.

(Karen smiles; David looks at her in astonishment.)

David: You know, Karen, that's the thing about you that I can't understand! You have such a sweet spirit about everything even when you are treated cruelly and unfairly. What is your secret?

Karen: It is no secret, David. It's just that — well — I'm a Christian!

David: And being a Christian makes you clean and sweet inside?

(Karen nods.)

David: I don't know, Karen. It's just like — well — like your mind and your heart are just kinda shampooed! You're not like other people! Do you know what I mean?

Karen (shyly): I think so!

David: Karen, what does it really mean when you say that you're a Christian? Why does that make such a difference in your life? I always thought that being a Christian only involved going to Sunday school and church. But I do that — and it hasn't changed my life like yours!

Karen: Well — David — being a Christian does involve more than that! You see, being a Christian is a personal relationship that each of us has to have with Christ. Nothing can change that. It's — well — our pastor calls it being "born again"!

(David looks bewildered.)

David: Born again?

Karen: You see, David, we all have to have a spiritual birth — we have to be born into the family of God! For when we are born into this world — we have a — a dead spiritual nature and because of it — we cannot be children of God. But when we are born again — we are taken in as children of God!

David: Now wait a minute! Dead spiritual nature! What do you mean?

Karen: Our pastor preached a sermon on the new birth last night. He explained it like this. When God created man, He had a wonderful plan in mind. There was direct communion between man and God. But, in this plan, God made one provision. He didn't want man to love Him and to serve Him because He had no other choice — and so He allowed man the privilege of loving Him and living with Him—or turning from His love and His companionship to choose another way. This choice was given by His placing one tree in the garden which He asked Adam and Eve not to touch. But, tempted by Satan, Adam and Eve ate of the forbidden tree and the punishment which God had promised as a penalty—spiritual death—was inflicted.

And since that time, every person born into the world has this dead spiritual nature as a result of the *choice* that our foreparents made back in the Garden of Eden. That is why it is necessary that you — and me — and everyone — be born again! Otherwise, we cannot be members of the family of God!

David: How does one receive the second birth?

Karen: David, I'm not too good at explaining all of this.

David: You're doing fine! I'm right with you! Now — how could I receive the second birth?

Karen: Well — when you were born into the physical world we know — you, of course, had no say in your destiny. In the spiritual world, however, you, alone, can determine your destiny. You either *accept* or *reject* the love of God which offers the new birth to you! We, in no way, are worthy of this new birth for our foreparents deliberately chose death and separation from God. But — because of His great love, God made another plan. Jesus came to earth and took our punishment upon Himself — and through His blood — we can be born again into the family of God!

David: How does one accept the new birth, Karen?

Karen: The first step is to accept the fact that you are a sinner — completely unworthy of God's love or favor. Undeserved as it is, God has offered His love and mercy to all mankind. But you have to accept Him and His love. Jesus died on the cross for you — and for me! He suffered that we might have eternal life — but it's up to us to accept or reject His great divine love. He paid the greatest price possible for you — and for me! (Karen's voice is filled with reverence as she speaks. They are both silent for a moment.)

David: But Karen, I don't really understand the fact that I am such a great sinner! I'm no gilded saint — but — I'm not so bad! I have never lied, stolen, drunk beer, murdered — those are the things that are sin, aren't they?

Karen: No, David. Those things are the results of sin! Sin first came into the world when Lucifer, the archangel of heaven plotted in his heart to take the place of the Almighty God. Then, of course, he was banished from heaven. Later, Adam and Eve ate of the forbidden fruit in the Garden of Eden and were cast out.

Since that time, everyone is born with the root of sin in his heart. These things you mentioned — lying, stealing, drinking, murder — came from that root. The initial sin — of which we are all guilty — is our complete forgetfulness of God — the ignoring of such divine love, the deliberate rejection of His grace.

David: Yeah — I see that now! I'm a sinner!

(He sits for a moment in deep thought.)

David: And accepting that fact, I can come to Jesus Christ and believe upon Him and He will give to me the new birth? And I will become a member of the family of God? Even though I am completely unworthy?

Karen: Yes, David.

David: But Karen — it is so simple!

Karen: Yes, David, it is simple — and it is for us all!

(There is a slight pause.)

Karen: We cannot begin to comprehend the love that Christ had for us when He allowed Himself to take upon Himself the plan of salvation and came to earth to live, to suffer and to die that we might be redeemed!

David: Truly there could be no greater love!

(They sit for a moment in silence.)

Karen: David, there is a picture in our church which I would like very much for you to see. I believe that it can explain the wonder of the love of Christ and of the word "redeemed" much better than I ever could! Would you like to go with me to see it?

David: Yes, I would, Karen. I would like that very much.

(They stand.)

(Curtain.)

SCENE II

The scene opens on the empty stage with the drape easel holding the picture *Christ on the Cross* by Rubens. Soft organ music should be playing *When I Survey the Wondrous Cross* backstage. The spotlight should be placed on the picture and all other lights dimmed.

After a moment, David and Karen enter. They stand to one side of the stage, studying the picture. They should be very serious and moved with feeling — but they should only be a part of the scene. The central focal point should be upon the picture itself.

Voice: Calvary!

40

Golgotha — it was called by some. Golgotha: the place of the skull!

Three blood-soaked prisoners stood huddled together. Three dark heavy crosses were stretched out upon the ground. Soldiers took the prisoners and forced their aching bodies to fit the crosses and then, with heavy blows, nailed them to the splintery wood.

The crosses, bearing their throbbing burdens, were then hoisted upward and dropped into the open holes prepared for them. There they hung, suspended between heaven and earth. And on the center cross hung a Man with a shining halo about His head. Here hung the Son of God.

The jealous and malicious high priest and his scheming father-in-law, Annas, had, at last, achieved their purpose. Jesus, the Christ, hung suspended between heaven and earth dying the most shameful death of all time.

Caiaphas stood on the hard ground and smiled in triumph.

One of the two thieves hanging on either side of Jesus looked, and through his pain-filled eyes he saw the halo. He whispered through parched lips: "Lord, remember me when You shall come into Your kingdom."

And then — the Man on the center cross smiled. He looked at the man at his side in loving compassion.

He answered: "This day you shall be with Me in Paradise!"

Caiaphas frowned. Even now, Christ offered salvation to dying men!

Time passed. And He hung upon the cross and suffered the greatest agony known to mankind. But — as He hung there, He looked down through the centuries and He saw you — He loved you — and He felt that you were worth this — the supreme price — the greatest manifestation of His love for you!

Greater love hath no man than this!

(Soloist sings *When I Survey the Wondrous Cross,* by Isaac Watts.)

> When I survey the wondrous cross
> On which the Prince of Glory died,
> My richest gain I count but loss,
> And pour contempt on all my pride.
>
> Forbid it, Lord, that I should boast,
> Save in the death of Christ, my God!
> All the vain things that charm me most,
> I sacrifice them to His blood.
>
> See from His head, His hands, His feet,
> Sorrow and love flow mingled down;

Did e'er such love and sorrow meet,
Or thorns compose so rich a crown?

Were the whole realm of nature mine,
That were a present far too small;
Love so amazing, so divine,
Demands my soul, my life, my all.

(David goes and kneels in front of the picture. Soloist repeats the last verse.)

Leader, take charge.

TRAGEDY OF COWARDICE

Characters

Rapphiel: the rich young ruler (Much care should be taken in casting this part for the success of the skit is dependent upon his ability to handle the lines.)

Anna: his mother

John: beloved disciple of Christ

Setting

Both scenes should take place in the garden of Rapphiel, the rich young ruler. If backdrops are available, picture a massive, elegant home with huge columns, etc. The garden setting should be as elaborate as possible. A fountain, palm trees (borrow potted ones from a nursery), floral arrangements, etc., should be in abundance. It would be well to have the floor covered with artificial grass.

Costuming

Anna should be dressed in heavy brocade with her hair piled on top of her head. She should wear many bracelets, rings, ear rings, etc. Rapphiel should wear a robe made of silk or velvet with a fur lined mantle. He should wear impressive rings and, perhaps, a gold chain about his shoulders. John should be dressed extremely plain and simple — but very neat.

Properties

There should be a silver tea service for the first scene.

Skit

SCENE I

(Rapphiel and Anna are seated in the garden. Anna is pouring tea into two cups on the tray as the curtain opens. She hands a cup to Rapphiel and then takes one for herself.)

Rapphiel: Thank you, Mother.

Anna (smiling): And thank you, my son, for your company this afternoon!

(Rapphiel laughs.)

Rapphiel: You are charming, Mother dear! What other woman in all of the land of Israel would think to thank her own son for his company! But I must say that I like it!

(Rapphiel sips his tea.)

Rapphiel: Oh! — I have forgotten to tell you! I saw John the other day!

Anna: John? John — the son of Zebedee?

Rapphiel: None other!

Anna: Well, what a surprise! Whatever is he doing here? And why hasn't he come to see us?

Rapphiel: First question: He's here with his Master!

Anna (putting up her hand in protest): Rapphiel! Don't say that! It makes him sound like a slave!

Rapphiel (grins): Well — if he is, he is the happiest slave I've ever seen! (He sobers.) No — he isn't a slave, Mother! John lives for this Christ — because he loves Him so much. Now question two: He hasn't been to see us yet because he has been terribly busy!

Anna: Busy? What does he do, Rapphiel?

Rapphiel: Well — I'm not altogether sure. I know that he does some speaking himself — and even some healing!

Anna: Healing? John?

Rapphiel: John! But his Master — this Jesus — is reputed to be the most eloquent of all speakers — and the greatest healer! Reports have it that He has even raised people from the dead. John goes everywhere with Him and assists with the crowds.

Anna: Do many people follow this Jesus, Rapphiel?

Rapphiel: People say that thousands of people follow Him everywhere He goes! But we weren't discussing this Jesus — we were discussing John! He sent you his love and promised to come to see us as soon as he could possibly get away.

(Anna smiles.)

Anna: That's nice. John is such a dear boy! I always loved him as though he were my own!

(Anna sobers, frowns a moment as she studies her teacup.)

Anna: Rapphiel — have you ever seen this Jesus?

Rapphiel: No, I haven't. I've heard a lot about Him — but I have never seen Him nor heard Him.

Anna: They say He is the Son of God. Do you believe that, Rapphiel?

Rapphiel: Nonsense! Mother, you know that you can't believe everything you hear!

Anna: Do you think you can know for sure that it is nonsense?

Rapphiel: Mother, don't be so silly! I can't discuss this man intelligently because I have never even seen Him.

Anna (musingly): But John must think Him to be the Son of God! Otherwise — why would he give up so much to follow Him? And even if he did think Him to be the Christ — would it be worth the price?

(Rapphiel laughs and arises. He places his cup on the tray.)

Rapphiel: That, my mother, is the great question of all times! I must be going! I am to be at a meeting of the Young Pharisees in an hour or so. (He bows.) I did so enjoy your company, Mother!

Anna: Oh, Rapphiel! Quit playing! I do enjoy your company. Very much! Why shouldn't I tell you so?

Rapphiel: You should — every time you think of it!

(He kisses her lightly.)

Rapphiel: I'll see you later, Mother.

Anna: All right, Rapphiel. Have a nice time!

(Rapphiel exits left. Anna sits, toying with her tea cup and thinking deeply.)

Anna: It would be a great question, wouldn't it? A great question!

(Curtain)

Scene II

(The stage is empty when the curtains open. After a few moments, Rapphiel walks onto stage with drooping shoulders and bowed head. He holds this side pose in the center of the stage for a moment. His right hand which faces the audience opens and shuts nervously. John enters after a time and stands quietly watching Rapphiel.)

John: Good day, Rapphiel.

(Rapphiel turns, startled. He looks at John for a long moment before speaking.)

Rapphiel: John!

(He drops his eyes and his shoulders sag. After a moment, he looks up at John.)

Rapphiel: You know?

(John nods and steps closer to Rapphiel.)

John: I know — but Rapphiel — it isn't too late!

(Rapphiel searches John with his eyes a moment.)

Rapphiel: Yes — it is, John.

(John steps closer with hand outstretched.)

John: Rapphiel —

Rapphiel: John — (he glances about stage and then smiles wanly) have a chair. Let me tell you — let me tell you!

44

(John sits.)

Rapphiel: John, I was on my way to a meeting of the Young Pharisees when I saw the crowd. Mother and I had been discussing you — and the price you had paid to follow this (he takes a deep breath)—to follow Christ! It was on my mind—and so when I saw the crowds, I decided to satisfy my curiosity as to what His teaching is really all about! So—I stopped!

The moment I saw Jesus, John, I knew deep within my heart that He was the Son of God. I knew — He didn't have to say a word. I just knew!

(John nods in understanding.)

Rapphiel: And so I stood and listened to words from heaven! My heart surged and yearned to know more — to experience more — to understand more! I knew that He possessed the eternal truth of life everlasting!

When He had finished speaking — I went to Him and said, "Good Master, what good thing shall I do that I may have eternal life?"

He looked at me, John — and He loved me!

(Rapphiel's voice breaks; his eyes are filled with agony.)

Rapphiel: He loved me! I knew that!

And then He said: "If thou wilt enter into life, keep the commandments!"

(Rapphiel grins ruefully.)

Rapphiel: That was easy enough. I answered: "Which?" Jesus said: "Thou shalt do no murder, thou shalt not commit adultery, thou shalt not steal. Honor thy father and thy mother and, thou shalt love thy neighbor as thyself." I said: "Master, all of these things have I kept from my youth up: what lack I yet?"

(Rapphiel turns from John and walks to the other end of the stage. He stands for a moment with bowed head. When he turns and comes back to John, suffering should be evident.)

Rapphiel: And then Jesus said: "If thou wilt be perfect, go and sell that thou hast, and give to the poor, and thou shalt have treasure in heaven: and come and follow me!"

(Rapphiel sits and puts his head in his hands.)

Rapphiel: And I turned — and went away!

John: Why, Rapphiel?

(Rapphiel throws out his hands.)

Rapphiel: You know the answer — but you're too kind to say it! I turned away from the Master because I am a coward! I knew the proposition that Christ was giving to me! His eyes searched me out! They were kind and loving — but they plumbed the depths of my soul! The issue that He presented to me was not that my giving away my wealth would be so important to others! The issue was my wealth's importance to me! His challenge to me, John, was to crucify myself, surrender myself and my selfish desires and aims, abandon them all for Him and for His plan!

John: That plan which Christ has for your life is such a beautiful one, Rapphiel! With your youth, your purity, your ability — you could make such a great contribution to the world in which we live.

(Rapphiel studies John a moment, takes a deep shuddering breath, arises and paces the stage.)

Rapphiel (with clenched hands): I can't, John! I can't!

(John arises and goes to stand behind him.)

John: Rapphiel, if you will dare to lose yourself — you will find a much better self in Christ!

Rapphiel: If I dare! (He turns to face John.) If I dare!

(He walks back to the chair and stands with his hands gripping its back.)

Rapphiel: John, I understand that. If I will deny myself the foolish, trivial things of idleness, security, and power, I will be free to love — to invest my life where it will compound itself into blessing to all about me — and to myself here and throughout eternity. I can find fulfillment — if I dare to lose myself!

(He stands with his head down. After a few moments, he looks up through pain-filled eyes.)

Rapphiel: But I can't because (vehemently) I'm a coward! I'm a coward! Without the armor of riches, I don't have the nerve to face life! (He pounds the top of the chair. There should be much feeling here.) I am a slave (bitterly) to myself!

(There is a moment here as Rapphiel sorts out the decision that he has made in his mind. He should portray suffering, regret, sorrow, and self-contempt in his actions. John watches him suffering too, longing to help.)

Rapphiel: To the greatest challenge of all time — the challenge to forsake self — and — and to find life in all of its fullness — to this great challenge, I turned away sorrowful. I turned away because I did not have the courage or the strength of character to *dare* to lose myself and find it in Someone bigger than I. I turned away from the Christ who loves me because — I — am — a coward!

(Curtain)

Leader: As in that generation of long ago when Jesus offered abundant life to a rich young ruler — so He stands today offering life to you! His challenge is to youth who will *dare* to choose and live for the "hard right over the easy wrong!" The youth in our skit, Rapphiel, made the wrong choice because, by his own testimony, he did not have the courage or the strength of character to become a Christian! Each youth, who has felt the beckoning call of Christ, understands that He will bring to them fulfillment, joy and peace. That is not the issue. The issue is the same which the rich young ruler faced: Do you have the courage to *dare* to lose yourself to find it again in Someone bigger than yourself?

The tragedy of cowardice is the greatest in the world. It takes your youth, your purity, your ability, your dreams and destroys them, leaving you — as it did Rapphiel — with only a broken heart and self-contempt.

The youth with real courage, real strength of character, real manhood and womanhood — can respond eagerly, willingly to Christ's great challenge.

(If desired, at this point, you could have a male soloist sing offstage the first verse of *Are Ye Able?* by Earl Marlatt. At the conclusion of the verse, two teens could come out in front of the curtain and sing a duet of the chorus. The fifth verse could be sung by soloist and the duet sing the chorus after which the invitation could be presented. This hymn could be continued as the invitation number, or the hymn *Have Thine Own Way, Lord* could be used. The words of *Are Ye Able?* are given below.)

"Are ye able," said the Master,
"To be crucified with Me?"
"Yea," the conquering Christians answered,
"To the death we follow Thee."

Chorus:
Lord, we are able, Our spirits are Thine,
Remold them, make us like Thee, divine:
Thy guiding radiance above us shall be
A beacon to God, To love and loyalty.

"Are ye able?" still the Master
Whispers down eternity,
And heroic spirits answer,
Now, as then in Galilee.

Chorus:
Lord, we are able, Our spirits are Thine,
Remold them, make us like Thee, divine:
Thy guiding radiance above us shall be
A beacon to God, To love and loyalty.

COME HOME!

Characters

James: prodigal son
Father: loving parent
Slick: companion of James
Waiter

Setting

The first scene takes place in the home of James's father. The room is furnished nicely but not lavishly. The second scene takes place in a small restaurant. There may be only one table at which James and Slick are sitting and a potted palm on either side in back of them indicating that other tables are beyond — or more tables may be arranged, if desired. The third scene takes place upon an empty stage.

Costuming

In the first scene, James should be dressed in casual, modern dress. His father wears a suit in both first and third scenes. In the second scene, James could only make a quick change of shirts. He wears the same costume in the third scene. The waiter is dressed in white.

Properties

A Bible, a check book, and a fountain pen will be needed in the first scene. In the second scene, there are two glasses on the table and two coke bottles. A letter will be needed for the waiter.

Skit

SCENE I

(The scene opens with James standing before the chair in which his father sits, reading the Bible.)

James: Father, please listen to the way I feel! I want to clear out of here!

Father: The devil is a hard taskmaster, my son. He can only lead you into trouble and bring you regret and heartache.

James: Father, I'm young! I want to get out and see what life is all about! I need to sow some wild oats, you know!

Father: Sow to the wind and you will reap the whirlwind. James, you have no idea the tragedy that sin can bring into your life!

(James throws out his hands in a gesture of impatience.)

James: Father, I'm young!

Father: And because you are young, your future is filled with golden promise which the devil will try to ruin.

(Father sighs and lays the Bible on a table.)

Father: But, James, it is your life. You will have to decide what you will make of it.

James: I have decided! I want to go and live it up! I want to fill my life with fun and excitement! I want to have all of the thrills that can be had in the world! I have always been sheltered, protected! I don't want that! I want to know life!

Father: You will find the thrills and the excitement are very shallow, my son. Sin offers to you the glittering things — the enticing things — and then when you have sold your manhood for them, you discover that they are only a sham. They do not satisfy. And you are left mangled, broken, and alone in darkness.

James: Darkness? Father, you have never seen the beauty of all the bright lights!

Father: But after awhile, the bright lights go out, my son — and you will find yourself in the night of sin! It is always night when you go without God!

James: You're of another generation! You don't understand what it is to be young now! How much there is to know! Come on, Father—give me my inheritance—and let me go out!

(He walks toward the front of the stage and throws out his arms in expectancy.)

James: Let me go out and *live!*

Father: James, you will not find life in that direction.

(He looks at James pleadingly for a moment. Then, he sighs heavily. He picks up the checkbook.)

Father: Are you certain that this is your choice — your final choice, my son?

James (eagerly): Yes — yes — it is my choice!

(Father sadly writes a check. James watches him happily. Father tears the check out of the book and holds it out to James.)

Father: James, you have made the decision. I could not make it for you. But James — remember this — you are my son and I love you! And when you are tired of the sham — you may always know that I love you and that you are always wanted at home!

(James takes the check. He folds it and places it in his pocket. He stands for a moment indecisively and then hastily bends and kisses lightly the top of his father's head.)

James: Thanks, Father! And — good-by!

(Father stands and looks at him longingly.)

Father: Good-by my son — and remember that my love is always with you — and you are always welcome at home!

(James looks at his father a moment, drops his eyes, turns, and exits left. Father stands looking after him with love and longing in his eyes.)

(Curtain)

Scene II

(The scene opens with James sitting at the table. He holds a glass in his hand. Slick is with him.)

Slick: And so — then — she said — get this now, James — then she said: I can cook too! (He slaps his knee, laughing uproariously.) Isn't that a scream?

(James laughs.)

James: That's pretty good, Slick, pretty good!

Slick: Sure it is, man! That's my profession — telling funny stories, living it up — and having a good time!

(James sits for a moment in deep, serious thought.)

Slick: What's the matter, Toddle Boy? Don't go serious on me! I'll have to vanish! I just can't live in an atmosphere of gloom!

James: You are my friend, aren't you, Slick?

Slick: Well — I like to laugh with you — and spend your money! Why do you ask?

James: Slick — I — I don't have any more money!

Slick: You don't have any money? What do you mean?

James: I mean just that! The bank foreclosed on my car this morning. Creditors are screaming down my neck — and there just isn't any more money in my account. Slick, what am I to do?

Slick: Well — now I'm sorry to hear that! Real sorry! Because — I not only can't live in an atmosphere of gloom — I can't live long in an atmosphere without money! That kind of atmosphere just makes me vanish!

James: Slick — if you're my friend, you'll help me!

Slick: Listen, kid, you got me all wrong! You — and money — are real fine! But — without money — I'm not sure I even remember your name!

James (intensely): Slick, you've got to help me! Advise me! What am I going to do?

Slick: I don't know, Toddle Boy. But whatever it is — it'll be without me!

James: Oh — I never should have come here! I never should have come here!

Slick: I agree with you!

James: But what am I going to do? Don't you realize that I need your friendship and your help?

Slick (exaggerated mockery): I am so sorry! It just breaks my heart! You see, Toddle Boy, I offer the laughs and the good times as long as you can finance the arrangement. But when the lights go off — and things begin to get dark — then that's where I get off!

(He stands.)

Slick: Toodle-oo, Toddle Boy! It was fun while it lasted!

(He leans down and speaks in a stage whisper.)

Slick: But it never lasts very long!

(Slick exits.)

James: What shall I do? I have squandéred all of my money! I have gone into sin! I have given my youth, my purity — everything into having a thrill! And now — now that I've sold out — now that my money is gone — I'm thrown away like a dirty rag!

And all of this time, I have been miserable inside! Even when the lights were bright and Slick — and all of the rest — were laughing it up — inside my heart, there was a dull ache! And now — here I sit — a complete failure! No job! No money! No friends! No home! Nothing! Nothing but the broken pieces of my dreams and my life! I am left with only the shattered pieces!

(Waiter comes on stage. He carries letter.)

Waiter: Are you James Stone?

James: Yes, I am.

Waiter: This just arrived for you.

(James take the letter.)

James: Thank you.

(He tears open the letter hurriedly and reads aloud.)

James: My son: This is a note to tell you that I love you and I am waiting anxiously for you to come back home!

(His hands drop to the table and he looks bewildered.)

James: My father!

(He looks at the letter in his hands incredulously.)

James: "I love you and I am waiting anxiously for you to come back home." I scorned his advice; I took his money! I squandered it all in riotous living! I went deep into things evil and wrong! I should be completely banished from the family forever! He should never allow me to see his face again. I have sinned! I, of my own choice, turned away from his love — and yet he still loves me! He loves me — and he is waiting anxiously for me to come back home!

(He looks at the letter in his hands.)

James: I am so unworthy of his love! Can I possibly return now? I am not worthy to be called his son — to live with him — to share his love! I am so unworthy!

(He studies the letter a moment and then his hands drop back to the table.)

James: Yet he loves me — still he loves me! And he wants me to come back home!

51

(He sits a moment in deep study.)

Father (offstage): My son, I love you and I am waiting anxiously for you to come back home!

(James looks up with sudden determination.)

James: I will go to my father! I will go home!

(He stands a moment looking at the letter in wonderment.)

(Curtain)

SCENE III

(The stage is empty when the curtains open. Father comes on stage and stands looking into the distance. After a moment, he bows his head in an attitude of prayer. After a few moments, James comes on stage. He stands, looking hesitantly at his father. Father raises his eyes and sees James. He looks at him a moment in unbelieving joy and then runs to him and gathers him to his heart in a strong embrace.

Father: Welcome home, my son! Welcome home!

(They hold this pose.)

Leader: The Word of God tells us that "Love Never Faileth." God's love is like that of the father whom we see depicted here in this skit. We, as free moral agents, many times, choose to trample under feet God's wonderful love and goodness to us. We forget so completely so often that "In Him we live and move and have our being." We forget that we are created in the image of God and that purpose for which we were created is for companionship with our Heavenly Father — and only through that fulfillment of companionship and close communion with Him can we find peace, joy and dreams come true!

Frequently, we take our lives into our own hands and live only in trying to satisfy selfish desires and ambitions until we almost destroy the image of God within our lives! And then we feel that we can never return to our Heavenly Father because we are so unworthy!

But God stands, as does the father of this skit, with wide open, loving arms ready and waiting to take back His wayward child and give to Him complete forgiveness and the fullness of His eternal love!

God, our Heavenly Father, stands now — asking *you,* His child, to turn from your wicked way — to accept His love — to return to the fold of His home.

(Curtain)

Invitation

WHAT PRICE — YOUR BEST?

Characters

Pilate: Roman Governor
Claudia: his wife
Leah: her maid
Messenger

Setting

The setting is in the sitting room of Pilate and his wife. This should be very lavish and as richly furnished as possible. A carpet would give atmosphere to the scene. Velvet drapes and plush pillows will be appropriate. Have a couple of chairs and at least one reclining couch for Claudia.

Costuming

Pilate and Claudia are both dressed elegantly in silks and velvets. They both should wear prominent, flashy jewelry. Leah should be barefoot and dressed in a very simple gown. Her hair should fall down her back. The Messenger should be in army uniform.

Properties

A scroll from which Leah reads should be available. Isaiah 53 should be printed upon the scroll. A piece of parchment will be needed for the Messenger.

Skit

SCENE I

(The scene opens with Leah standing to the side of the reclining couch on which Claudia is lounging. All is still except for her even voice. Claudia is listening intently.

Leah. "He is despised and rejected of men; a man of sorrows and acquainted with grief: and we hid as it were our faces from him; he was despised and we esteemed him not.

"Surely he hath borne our griefs and carried our sorrows: yet we did esteem him stricken, smitten of God and afflicted.

"But he was wounded for our transgressions ——"

(There is the sound of loud footsteps offstage.)

Pilate (offstage): Out of my way, man! Can't you clean that floor some other time?

(Pilate enters noisily. Leah stands looking at him through frightened eyes, hesitantly folds the scroll together awaiting further word from her mistress.)

Pilate: Whatever have I done to deserve being pushed off to rule over a poor little colony like this — one that is filled with disruptions and hatred — and — oh!

(He looks at Claudia in a speechless rage.)

Claudia: Pilate, what is the matter now?

(She turns to Leah.)

Claudia: You may go now.

(Leah lays down the scroll on a table and exits.)

Pilate: Oh — you know — there was this silly uprising the other day! I now discover that Caesar has become tired of so much disputing down here — and so he has sent me word that if he receives one more complaint — I will be in imperial disfavor!

Claudia: So?

Pilate: So! He doesn't know what these people are like! It's an impossibility! A Roman can't win their favor or respect regardless of what he might do!

Claudia: Have you tried?

Pilate: Yes, I've tried!

(He throws himself onto a chair.)

Pilate: Well! Forget it!

Claudia (laughs): Are you giving that advice to me — or to yourself?

(Pilate grins.)

Pilate: You don't seem to be overly upset — so I guess that advice goes to me!

Claudia: I have learned not to be upset over passing things!

Pilate (sarcastic): Passing things like the Imperial favor?

Claudia (unperturbed): Passing things like the Imperial favor! Those are earthly things! (She leans forward earnestly.) There are values that are eternal, Pilate!

(Pilate reaches to the table and picks up the scroll which Leah has laid there.)

Pilate: So — you have been hearing the Jewish Bible again?

(There is a knock at the door.)

Pilate: Come in.

(Messenger enters. He hands the parchment to Pilate. Pilate takes it, tears it open and flings it to the floor in anger. He glares at the Messenger. The Messenger returns his gaze unconcerned.)

Messenger: Do you have an answer, sir?

(Pilate rises and glares at him.)

Pilate: Yes, I have an answer!

(He sits down and gives a long sigh of defeat.)

Pilate: Tell Caiaphas that I will have the hearing — and that I agree to hear the case out of doors so they won't have to pollute themselves by entering the house of a Gentile! (He looks up.) Bring me word when they arrive.

(Messenger bows and exits. Pilate throws the parchment to the table.)

Pilate: What an impossible situation! I'm at the mercy of this slimy high priest, Caiaphas! When he makes a request — such as this — trying a man at this hour in the outer court — I have to give in! I have to give in!

Claudia: Why, Pilate?

(Pilate frowns in anger.)

Pilate: Because if there is one more uprising here ——

Claudia: You will lose Imperial favor! And Imperial favor is more important to you than anything else!

Pilate: What else is there?

Claudia: There is God!

Pilate: God! What do you know of God?

Claudia: Not as much as I want to know, Pilate. But I am learning and, Pilate, I believe that His Son is here — on earth! Oh, Pilate, if you could only learn the truth from Him!

Pilate: Truth? What is truth?

Claudia: Jesus Christ has the answer to that question. Pilate — would you go to Him — soon — and ask Him that? He could help you, Pilate. He could help you to see eternal things as they really are!

(Pilate rises and goes to her. He kneels by her and takes her hands in his.)

Pilate (softly): Claudia, the man whom I am to try tonight — is called Jesus the Christ!

Claudia: Pilate! No! How could it be?

Pilate: Those scheming high priests — Caiaphas and his father-in-law, Annas, have been after him for months! Years! They finally got someone to sell him out tonight — and they're bringing him here for trial!

Claudia (softly as if to herself): "He is despised and rejected of men: a man of sorrows, and acquainted with grief."

Pilate: What did you say?

Claudia: I was quoting some Scripture that was written long ago in the Jewish Bible by a man named Isaiah. It was a prophecy concerning the Son of God who would come to earth.

(Claudia looks at Pilate long, searchingly.)

Claudia: Pilate, what will you do with Jesus?

(Pilate drops his eyes. He breathes heavily. He looks up at Claudia, his eyes begging her to understand.)

Pilate: I'll do the best that I can for Him. I'm in a terrible spot!

You know that, Claudia! I'm in a terrible spot! But I'll do my best!

Claudia: Will you, Pilate?

(He looks at her a moment and then drops his head down upon his hands.)

Pilate: I'll try!

Claudia: Pilate, do you know what your best will be?

Pilate: Yes, Claudia, I know.

(There is a knock at the door.)

Pilate (raises his head): Come in.

(Messenger enters.)

Messenger: The High Priest, Caiaphas, is here, sir. He is waiting in the outer court.

(Pilate sighs heavily, gets to his feet, looks long at Claudia and then turns and follows the messenger from the room. Claudia watches them go and then bows her head in prayer.)

(Curtain)

Scene II

(When the curtain opens, there is a roar of jeering voices offstage. Frequently the words "Hail King of the Jews!" can be heard distinctly amid the hubbub. Claudia is on the couch; Leah is looking through the window.)

Leah: That was the last blow, my lady. They are finished with the chastisement now! He is still standing there quietly, unmoving. He is so — so serene!

(Claudia reaches for the scroll and opens it.)

Claudia: "He was oppressed and he was afflicted, yet he opened not his mouth: he is brought as a lamb to the slaughter, and as a sheep before her shearers is dumb, so he openeth not his mouth."

(The hubbub outside vanishes away.)

Leah: That does describe Him, doesn't it, my lady?

Claudia: Yes, Leah. It describes the Son of God!

(There is a moment's silence. Leah turns back from the window.)

Leah: They have taken him to Pilate!

(Claudia closes her eyes in an attitude of prayer.)

Leah: Pilate has tried to help Him, my lady. He found no cause in Him — at first!

Claudia (wearily): At first!

Leah: Then he sent Him to Herod. The mob wouldn't allow him to just let Him go! And then — when Herod refused to do anything, he told them that he would chastise Jesus — and then let Him go!

Claudia: But they wouldn't stand for that! And neither would Pilate!

Leah: Then he offered the freedom of Jesus against that of that

56

wicked murderer and robber, Barabbas. Why — I was so sure that they would never let Barabbas be set free! Pilate did all that he could for Jesus, my lady!

Claudia: Not all, Leah. He could have given himself!

Leah: Himself! But — my lady ——

(There are footsteps offstage. Leah steps back. Pilate enters. His whole body depicts defeat. He walks over and sits in a chair and hangs his hands between his knees. His head is bowed. Claudia nods to Leah. Leah exits.)

Pilate: I'm sorry, Claudia!

Claudia: Why?

(Pilate looks up, startled.)

Pilate: Why what?

Claudia: Why are you sorry?

(Pilate throws out his hands and then he arises and walks about the stage.)

Pilate: I tried, Claudia! You know I tried!

Claudia: Are you trying to convince me of something, Pilate — or yourself?

(Pilate sighs heavily.)

Pilate: All right. I knew the issue at stake, Claudia. I knew what it meant to give my best. And throughout the whole trial, I was miserably full of indecision. It was constantly battling in my heart: "If I release Him — I will lose my position! If I condemn Him — I will lose — (he bows his head) — the truth!

Claudia: And so you tried to save yourself and Him?

Pilate (nods): Yes.

(There is a moment's silence.)

Pilate: I tried, Claudia! But when they began to shriek: "We have no king but Caesar" — I lost! Because I knew then — that it was either me or Him! I would either have to be willing to lose myself to find Him — or lose Him to retain me! But — Claudia — what could I do? A man must live!

Claudia: Why? Jesus is willing to die! Jesus, the Son of God ——

(Pilate jumps to his feet. He glares at Claudia.)

Pilate: Don't say that!

Claudia: But it's true, Pilate! You know it is! You asked Him the meaning of truth — didn't you, Pilate — and you read the answer in His eyes! He is the truth — and the life! Why, then, should it be so hard for you to die out to self — to gain truth and life eternal?

(Pilate drops his eyes.)

Claudia: The loudly screamed charges of Caiaphas, the rabble cry of the mob, the chastisement — nothing was able to shake Him from His sublime consciousness of His mission! A love overwhelming and divine has brought Him here — and it will carry Him hence to an end that even you, Pilate, cannot change!

(Pilate sits. Claudia arises and stands beside him.)

Claudia: You had to make a decision tonight! A decision between Jesus Christ — and yourself! You had to choose your master! And because of your choice, you have lost eternal life — you have lost your self-respect — you have lost everything that is worthwhile — everything of value in this life and in the next! You have lost it all, Pilate! You have lost it! Because you chose yourself above Christ! Because you were afraid to give your best!

(Curtain)

Leader: What will *you* do with Jesus who is called the Christ? Invitation

TEENS TALK

Characters

Rev. Clark: pastor
Greg: teen-age boy
Shelia: teen-age girl
Special Guests: Deletta Vandegrift; Richard Spindle; Anne Bohlke; Dwayne Vaughn

Setting

The setting is in the office of Rev. Clark. This should include a desk and chairs for Rev. Clark, Greg, and Shelia. The setting should be made to look as much as possible like a minister's well-equipped study. The furniture should be to one side of the stage.

Costuming

Greg and Shelia will be in typical, teen-age dress. Rev. Clark should be dressed as becoming a minister. Deletta should be dressed in dressy type clothes; Richard should wear a suit; Anne should be dressed in an old fashioned costume. Dwayne should wear casual clothing.

Properties

The minister will need a "wadar set." This is a matchbox covered with paper. A dial should be placed on the top of the box with a brad so that the hands may be moved easily. There should be book, etc., on the pastor's desk. Music books will be needed for Deletta, a president's gavel for Richard, an old-fashioned fan for Anne, and a trumpet for Dwayne.

Skit

(The scene opens with Rev. Clark seated at his desk reading. A knock comes at the door. Rev. Clark looks up.)

Rev. Clark: Come in.

(Greg and Shelia enter.)

Rev. Clark: Oh, Greg, Shelia! Hello! (He stands.) It's so nice to see you!

(Rev. Clark and Greg shake hands.)

Rev. Clark: Won't you have a seat?

Shelia: Thank you, Rev. Clark.

(They all sit.)

Rev. Clark: That was quite a game you played Friday night, Greg.

Greg: Thank you, sir. I didn't do much!

Rev. Clark: I thought that you did a great deal! That last touchdown was spectacular. I'm sure that you agree with me, Shelia!

Shelia (smiles): Of course!

(There is a pause.)

Shelia: Rev. Clark, last night Greg and I listened very carefully to your sermon—and we want to be Christians! We really do! But—it's — it's just that — well, we're young — we want to have fun we well, we want to be popular! And if we become Christians, we will have to give up all of those things!

Greg: Yeah, that's our problem, Rev. Clark. You see — really and truly we want — in our hearts — to accept your challenge — and the challenge of Christ — to follow Him and to be really true Christian teens. But — well — like Shelia said — we feel that when we become Christians, we will have to give up all hope for popularity and fun!

Shelia: We wanted to explain to you our position.

Rev. Clark: I'm so happy that you did, Shelia. Because, you see, you are both very wrong in your belief!

Greg: No, Rev. Clark, we aren't wrong! I don't know of anyone who is really a Christian who has ever attained anything in life as a teen-ager. Oh — there's Archie who is a Christian — but he is such a square! We want to live rich, full lives — and we don't believe that we can and be Christians!

Rev. Clark: I understand your feelings, Greg. Do you know that this is one of the most effective weapons that the devil uses in his platform to defeat all teen-agers in their Christian experience? And like all of the devil's tales, it is completely false! Christianity enhances living; it enhances one's popularity and achievements rather than being a detracting factor. And when you know teens who blame their lack of popularity and achievements upon the fact that they are Christians, you can know that it is completely untrue. Let's consider a moment.

Being a Christian and living a clean life doesn't excuse us from doing the very best that we can do with all that we possess as an individual. We still need to read about etiquette, bettering our appearances, and improving ourselves socially. You see, doing your best outwardly is just a part of being Christians inwardly. And Archie's lack of doing his best outwardly will probably be the main reason for his being considered a "square."

Christianity brings real true joy to your life that you won't find anywhere else. But the devil so many times can defeat teen-agers with this one cruel falsehood.

Shelia: You call it a falsehood, Rev. Clark. Well — now that you mention it — Archie's being a Christian probably doesn't figure at all in his unpopularity — but Rev. Clark, honestly, I just can't believe that it can be done! I would love to be a Christian teen — if I thought that I could really enjoy life at the same time! But I have never known a teen-ager who has gotten all out of life that I would like — and has been a genuine Christian!

Rev. Clark: All right, Shelia. I am going to do away with that problem right now for I am going to introduce you to some teens who can disprove your statement. These are real live teen-agers facing the same problems, complexities, and temptations that you face. And each of them have proven the worth of Christianity in a teen-ager's life!

(He opens desk drawer and brings out "wadar set.")

Rev. Clark: This is called a "wadar set." It is a new invention and it allows me to bring anyone to my office whom I desire. So I am going to turn this dial (he does so as Greg and Shelia watch interestedly) and I am going to bring to our office a teen-age girl and let us listen to her testimony.

(Deletta enters. She smiles at Greg and Shelia.)

Rev. Clark: Greg, Shelia, this is Deletta Vandegrift. As you see, she is carrying some music books. She has reached the top of the ladder in high school music. She is a member of the All-state orchestra, has an excellent rating on her instrument: the viola. She also performs at various gatherings on the accordion and at the keyboard of the organ.

Athletically, she is a whiz! She plays on the high school tennis team and the volleyball team. And in spite of the hours spent on ball courts she is in the top of her school's "intelligentsia!"

Socially, Deletta scores top honors! She has served as president of the FHA, secretary of her class, and chosen only recently as "Personality Queen."

Shelia: Wow!

Rev. Clark: That isn't all! She is pianist of her local church, president of her Sunday school class, and has been awarded scholarships in both piano and voice and in academical attainments for college.

Greg: She measures up in achievements and popularity all right!

Rev. Clark: Yes, she does — and she also disproves the devil's theory that you cannot attain all of these things — and be a Christian. Give us your testimony, Deletta.

Deletta: At the age of six years, I first confessed my sins, and God gladly forgave them. An unestablished experience was mine for the devil beat me around with just such falsehoods until I was 16. But on the last night of the year, December 31, I made my consecration as thorough as I had knowledge to do so. I was committed to live for Christ regardless of the price.

The quotation: "If it is worth doing at all, it is worth doing right," has been a motto of mine throughout my teen-age years. Why not put all of myself into being a staunch Christian in soul, heart, spirit, personality, friendliness, leadership, talents, loyalty, and sincerity, as I had done in my school life? Through a deep devotion to Christ and a God-given determination, the problems and decisions of my my high school life have been solved under His leadership. I believe that I have not been able to attain these honors in spite of my religion — but I believe that I have attained each of them *because* of my religion. I am happier and lead a richer, fuller life now than I ever dreamed possible. It is because Christ is my Saviour!

My relationship with Christ is the most important and the most precious area in my life. This is the hub around which everything else revolves. And I know that I can find the fulfillment of my dreams in His will! I love Him supremely!

(Deletta exits. Greg and Shelia look at Rev. Clark in wonderment. He turns the dial on the "wadar set.")

Rev. Clark: That's only one! Let me introduce you to a boy — Richard Spindle.

(Richard enters. He smiles and nods at Greg and Shelia.)

Rev. Clark: Richard is tall, dark and handsome. He makes all of the boys like him; all of the girls sigh; and everyone respects him. He has taken just about every honor that high school can bestow. He has been chosen as class favorite, class treasurer, class vice-president for two years, and is now serving as senior class president. He has played leading roles in his junior class play and his senior class play. He has also excelled in declamation and in music. And he was only recently chosen by the entire student body of his high school as the boy "most likely to succeed!"

Greg: Quite a guy!

Rev. Clark: And he is very active in church, serving as Sunday school teacher, youth group president, and a frequently used soloist. He has captured the hearts of all who know him and has attained real prominence in his school and in his church. And he has done it as a consistent Christian teen! Listen to his testimony.

Richard: "The Lord is my light and my salvation, whom then shall I fear?" Truly this is the theme of my testimony. For the Lord is my light and my salvation, and with His glorious presence abiding near, I have no need to fear. The Lord has been the Guide of my life for a number of years. He has been my best Friend. He has led me through valleys which seemed to be utterly uncrossable. He has led me humbly over the mountaintops. Truly, He is the axis of my life. I am determined that "neither death, nor life, nor angels, nor principalities, nor powers, nor things present, nor things to come, nor height, nor depth, nor any other creature shall separate me from the love" of my God in Christ Jesus.

High school is a very happy period of life for me. I have many friends and have had a wonderful time during these four years of high school. And Christ has been my closest companion through it all. He has given me hope for the future. He has given me strength and wisdom for today. What more could one ask than to have Jesus Christ as his Guide? I am thrilled to be able to say: "Throughout my high school years, I have been a Christian teen — and God — and others — have honored my life and I have known joy untold!"

(Richard exits.)

Greg: Hmm! That was an eye-opener! He just about took over the works, didn't he?

Rev. Clark: Yes, Richard is most popular and enjoys fun in super abundance in his life.

(Rev. Clark picks up "wadar set" and moves the dial.)

Rev. Clark: Now, I'm going to introduce you to Anne Bohlke.

(Anne enters, smiles, and nods to Greg and Shelia.)

Rev. Clark: As you can tell by her costume, Anne is very interested in drama. Throughout her high school days, she has taken leading roles. She is a member of the National Thespians, Little Theatre, and has had leads in such plays as *Huckleberry Finn, Connecticut Yankee, Time Out for Ginger,* and *Antic Spring* in which she took state honors. She was class representative and is on the cabinet of Y-Teens, member of the FTA, Latin Club, reporter on her school paper, member of the choir, supreme court justice of the school, class treasurer, speech club president, and representative to the student council!

And in her church work, she serves as Sunday school teacher, secretary of the missionary group — and of her youth Sunday evening group.

Anne has reached excellence in every area of her life — including the spiritual. Anne, will you give to us your testimony?

Anne: I like to think of Jesus as a personal Friend — a Friend I can talk to! I can tell Him all about my problems and He always understands. He is a Friend who is interested in my joys and happiness. He is a dependable Friend — He is always at my side when I need Him most! He is genuinely interested in me and my life. He loves me and cares for me!

How can I help but love my wonderful Friend? How can I help but want to give my life for His service? How can I help but want to be more like Him? How can I help but want to be the kind of friend to Him — and to others — that He is to me?

My home is just a few blocks from the Mississippi River and, daily, we can hear the whistles of the steam boats as they push their barges before them up and down the river. A pilot stands behind the wheel. The course and destination of the boat are in his hands. Christ is the pilot of my life — its course and destination are in His hands!

I was in a motorboat on the river not long ago when, for no apparent reason, the motor quit. It refused to start and, as we had no oars, we drifted aimlessly downstream. I thought that this was like my life before I met Christ. I was drifting aimlessly — without a purpose to my life. Now my purpose is to live for Him. I am ready to go wherever He would have me to go and do whatever He would have me to do. I love my Saviour and my only desire is to do His complete will.

(Anne exits.)

Shelia: I am beginning to see how much the devil has been trying to hoodwink us into believing a real falsehood!

(Rev. Clark takes out "wadar set" and turns dial.)

Rev. Clark: I am so thrilled to know that you are beginning to understand this, Shelia. Let me introduce you to one more teen: Dwayne Vaughn.

(Dwayne enters. He smiles and nods to Greg and Shelia.)

Rev. Clark: Dwayne is a most unusual young man. He lives a rich, full life, is respected and loved by all who know him, and his consecration is deep and complete. In school, Dwayne is a member of the track team; has lettered two years in track and holds some of the school records. He is a member of the football team and has lettered for two years in the position of tackle. He is first chair trumpet in the school band and all-city band and is leader of the brass section. He has received first place in district and regional musical contests both in solo on the trumpet and in a brass ensemble. He also plays in the church orchestra and has been chosen to play for special evangelical campaigns. Although Dwayne has received recognition in many areas of his life, he possesses a complete commitment to the will of God. Let us listen to his testimony.

Dwayne: It was during the summer when the greatest moment of my life came to me. Oh, there have been other "big" moments in my life — but they all slip away into oblivion when I remember the moment I met Christ. Before that time, my heart had been wildly, madly searching for something. I wasn't satisfied with life. Somehow I felt that there must be more to life than I had discovered. And then — in the heat of an August night, I heard His whisper: "Come unto Me." His eyes seemed to search into the deepest recesses of my soul. I knew that my life would not be the same if I did choose to follow Him. I knew that I would surrender my selfish desires and live only for Him. And somehow, I also knew that my saying "yes" would involve my entering full-time Christian service for Christ and this does not offer a life of smug, easy complacent living. I knew the challenge of Christ is to a life filled with adventure, daring, and self-abandonment. I knew that my following His call would lead to temptations and times when I would have to stand alone — but I found in His Word the promise that if I would seek first the Kingdom of God and His righteousness that "all of these things" would be added unto me. And then — when I took my eyes off myself — and looked into His eyes — everything but His love fell away into utter insignificance. For I could see by the tenderness and kindness in His eyes the worthwhileness of the constant challenge of my living, victorious Christ! Christ cannot take weaklings who are concerned only for themselves! Instead — His challenge is to high resolve, to valiant living, to serving humbly and gloriously — for His sake!

I heard Him whisper: Come unto Me! My self grew dim. I followed after Him! He leads the way. He guides my steps. He holds my hand. He gives me joy and peace each day. I found life abundant when I answered His call.

Will *you* not follow when *you* hear Him call?

(Dwayne exits.)

Greg: Thank you, Rev. Clark, for introducing us to these fine Christian teen-agers. It has helped me to understand how the devil has been trying to cheat me out of salvation because of a lie that I would be denied my God-given desires. I am ready now to accept your challenge. I want to be a Christian teen.

(Greg and Shelia kneel.)

(Curtain)

Leader, take charge for the invitation.